SACRAMENTO'S MEMORIAL AUDITORIUM: SEVEN DECADES OF MEMORIES

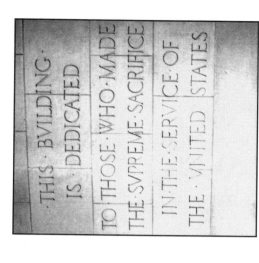

·THIS· BVILDING·
IS· DEDICATED
TO· THOSE· WHO· MADE
THE· SVPREME· SACRIFICE
IN· THE· SERVICE· OF
THE· VNITED STATES

SACRAMENTO'S MEMORIAL AUDITORIUM

SEVEN DECADES OF MEMORIES

BONNIE WEHLE SNYDER

PAULA J. BOGHOSIAN

Memorial Auditorium Book Project

Sacramento

This project has been funded by donations from the Sacramento Housing and Redevelopment Agency and MTS Incorporated (Tower Records/Books/Videos), and by a loan from Capital City Preservation Trust.

All proceeds from the sale of this book will be donated to the Memorial Auditorium Fund to further rehabilitate and enhance the usability and enjoyability of the Sacramento Memorial Auditorium.

Preliminary layout design by the Rakela Company, Sacramento, California.
Cover design by Tom Winter. Cover photo by Don Tateishi.
Graphic of building by KMD Architects, San Francisco.
Printed by Bertelsmann Industry Services, Valencia, California.

For information on ordering additional copies, please contact:

Memorial Auditorium Book Project
P.O. Box 191275
Sacramento, CA 95819

This book is dedicated to all of those who believe
the Sacramento Memorial Auditorium
is much more than a building—
that it is a treasure chest of cherished memories.

PREFACE

Sacramento is full of people who were born and raised here or who have lived here for the best part of their lives. For many of these people, the Memorial Auditorium holds special and significant memories. They think of the building in terms of the seminal events in their lives: their first prom, their high school graduation, watching boxing matches with their dad, or even registering and reporting there for evacuation to wartime internment camps. I am not one of these people. I moved to Sacramento in 1987, a year after the building was closed down. What business do I have then writing a book about the auditorium?

In fact, I may be the perfect person for the job. My first exposure to the building came when I joined Save The Auditorium in 1991. I visited the empty building and was awed by its size and magnificence even as it stood with its seats removed and various city property stored on the arena floor. I helped with the Measure H drive by collecting signatures and canvassing my neighborhood before the election. The thing that struck me most about doing those things was the response I so often got. Sacramentans' memories for the structure ran deep. Their memories were strong and very important to them. I began to feel I had really missed something, not having grown up here, and to envy Sacramentans for their good fortune at having an auditorium to which they felt so connected.

After the initiative passed, I was appointed to the Citizens' Advisory Committee overseeing the rehabilitation. I helped to decide what specific items to include in the project and to select the team to do the work. I made many more visits to the auditorium as the work progressed. I came to feel connected to the building in my own way, and it became very special and important to me, too.

The idea for a book came out of this experience. It emerged from discussions with friends about how I could help further the project. I began the book full of enthusiasm, and ended up the same way. Since I didn't know the building's history, it was all exciting news to me; since I had no experiences of my own attending events there, other people's stories fascinated me. I think the book has benefited as a result.

While I intended the book as a gift to the auditorium—and it is one—it also turned out being a gift to me. In the course of doing the research, I met some of the most interesting people I have ever known. I got to know many more people in Sacramento than I had known before, learned much more about the city, and came to feel even more connected with the building and its history. Although all of the proceeds from the book will go into a fund to continue the rehabilitation of the building, what I have gained from writing it is payment enough.

Paula's background was a perfect complement to mine. She has lived in Sacramento for many years and attended events at the auditorium. She worked on Sacramento architectural surveys and is extremely knowledgeable about the city's architectural history. She was also a member of the Turner Construction design/build team that undertook the rehabilitation, and as a result, became very intimate with the building and all its facets. In addition, she has belonged to several clubs and organizations that have introduced her to many of the movers and shakers in town. Her contacts were an invaluable base for getting information and making other contacts.

Bonnie Snyder
February 1997

ACKNOWLEDGEMENTS

O ver the course of this project, Paula and I interviewed or spoke with dozens of people to get information and insight about the auditorium. Dozens more were kind enough to give us or allow us to use their stories, photos, programs, or tickets. Others helped us with research and photography. The hard-working staff at the Sacramento Archives and Museum Collection Center (History Center) gave us invaluable assistance finding photographs and information in their files. We also got very able assistance from the staff at the California State Library and the Sacramento Public Library. Thus the project involved a community of people, which we think is especially fitting for a project involving a building that so definitely belongs to the Sacramento community. Unfortunately, we cannot begin to list here the numerous people who helped us. (There is a complete list is at the back of the book.) But we thank them all.

Some of those who helped gave many, many hours of their time and effort. Don Cox and Denise O'Connor spent days staring at microfilm to find articles about the auditorium and the many events that took place there. Amanda Meeker, Frank Lortie, and Francesca Smith also put in many hours at the library. Dennis Warren and Greg Savalin helped greatly by researching and printing many photos from their files. Ed Andersen and Don Tateishi donned hard hats and climbed around the building lugging cameras to take photographs for us. Ed printed and scanned numerous others. Don Cox and Tom Winter also spent weeks scanning photos. Tom designed the cover and the graphics inside. Don Cox also contributed the prologue and epilogue. Our editors, Heather Baker, Suzanne Mikesell, and John Snyder, pored over our manuscript for days to improve our product, while John, Don Cox, and Dorene Clement proofread the final draft for misplaced (or unplaced) commas, etc. The Rakela Company designed the layout and guided us through its implementation. Finally, Richard Tolmach stepped in and rescued us when the technical going got rough.

Without all these people, we could never have completed this project.

Bonnie Snyder

TABLE OF CONTENTS

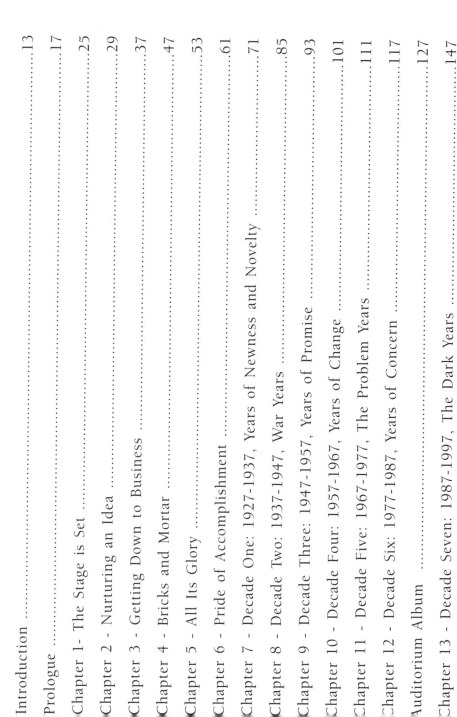

INTRODUCTION

The Sacramento Memorial Auditorium is not just one of the most striking pieces of architecture in the city. It is not just an auditorium, or a place to hold concerts, dances, circuses, festivals, etc. It is all of those things and more: For most people who grew up in Sacramento, it is a storehouse of cherished memories. It is the place where Sacramento gathered, where it dreamed, hoped, and fell in love, where it coalesced as a community and came of age.

When the building first opened in 1927, people flocked to the ceremony. There was standing room only long before the festivities began. Many who were turned away waited to get a glimpse of the beautiful new structure after everyone else had left. At the reopening in 1996, over 20,000 people attended the two-day open house. Many were brought to tears, and others nearly so, by the swell of nostalgia that washed over them as they revisited the building that had been closed for over ten years. The 1927 crowd approached the building with anticipation and hope. The 1996 crowd entered with those things overlaid by years of memories.

The crowd who came to the first opening later attended operas and concerts and saw famous stars whom they had previously had to go to San Francisco to enjoy. They donned formals and attended dances put on by local organizations. The generations that followed them listened to big bands and

attended dances sponsored by the USO. After the war, the music changed and so did the dances. Jazz and later rock'n'roll began to fill the auditorium and the dancing often took place in the aisles—sometimes even on the seats! Throughout the years there were sports, circuses, festivals, proms, and graduations in the auditorium. There, much of Sacramento's collective memory of pleasurable, important, life-changing experiences was formed.

While the building was closed and arguments were going on over what to do with it, a generation of Sacramento high school students missed one of the most memorable experiences their parents, or perhaps their older siblings or cousins had had—that of walking down an aisle formed by rows of students holding candles, toward their graduation on the stage in the Memorial Auditorium. Now, many high schools are returning to the auditorium for their graduations. New memories are being made.

In the 1920s Sacramentans worked hard to get the Memorial Auditorium and then argued over where to put it. Since then, it has been the subject of several other controversies that enliven this story. But that's not surprising. People get very worked up about things that are important to them. This building, which brought so much to Sacramento and which holds so much of its heart, is very important to its people. The Memorial Auditorium's story is interesting, funny, human. It is a story that had to be told.

Sixteenth and J Streets looking east, a few years after the Memorial Auditorium opened.
Eugene Hepting Collection, Sacramento Archives and Museum Collection Center.

PROLOGUE

hank you, Jennifer, dear for bringing me to the auditorium today to see all the renovation work they've done here. You know, this old building has played a big part in my life over the years. I graduated from high school right here in this building way back in '31. I've been to the opera, and to musicals, why, I even came to a boxing match once. Your grandpa and I used to come to dances here, when we were just courting. And I can remember taking your mother to see the Nutcracker every year at Christmastime.

The thing that always sticks in my mind the most, though, was that opening night. What an evening that was! It was February 22, nineteen and twenty-seven. The show was scheduled to start at 8:00 p.m., but we hoped to get a good seat, so like most others in town we arrived early—'bout six o'clock if I remember correctly—and it was a good thing we did too, because a lot of others had the same idea. In the days before the opening it seemed the whole town was all excited, and it was about all anyone talked about. It seemed like the whole town was going to be there, and it darn near was. I remember reading in the newspaper the next day that there were six thousand people there that night, and there were thousands more turned away at the door. 'Course many of those came back after the performances just to walk about and get a look at the new auditorium.

And, you know, that was back when there was only about a hundred thousand people in all of Sacramento!

It was kind of chilly when we arrived, and it had been raining off and on—just a typical February. I remember the smell of the dampness roiling up off the street and the sounds of horns honking as everybody hurried to the plaza entrance. A lot of people were already lined up at the front door. I turned and looked back at Pop, and he smiled and waved as he drove off in our new Pontiac. It was shiny black, one of those big boxy squared-off cars that you see in all those gangster movies. My brother, Thomas, used to brag about what a powerful engine it had. We bought it from Harvey Whitten who used to have a dealership right over there at 16th and K.

Anyway, Pop dropped me and Thomas and Momma off, and went to find a place to park. I was about twelve, Thomas about ten, and we had an older sister, Martha, 'bout sixteen I think, and she was singing in the chorus that night.

As we waited, I remember thinking how pretty Momma looked. She was dressed in this three-piece suit that was all matching: a blouse, skirt and what we used to call a redingote—kind of a long, loose coat. She was also wearing a hat called a cloche, 'cause it was kind of bell shaped. 'Course you couldn't re-

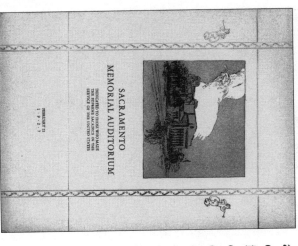

Cover and pages of the opening night program, February 22, 1927. Additional pages listed city officials, the Honor Roll of Veterans, and the words to some songs.

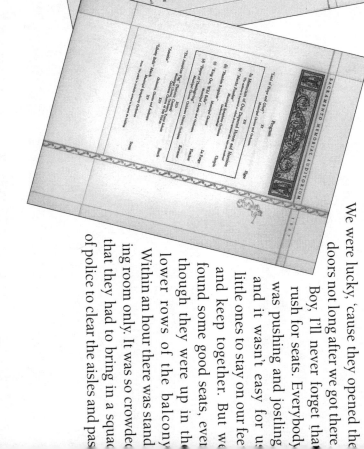

ally see her outfit too well, 'cause she had her wool coat on over it, but I think that suit cost her about fifteen dollars, and that was a lot of money in those days. My, how things change. I still have a snapshot of her that evening that Thomas took with his box camera while we were waiting in line. I also kept a copy of that evening's program. Remind me to show it to you sometime.

As Pop walked up to us he was smoking his pipe. He looked mighty handsome too, in his dark wool over-coat, and his black fedora with the wide satin band.

Under the coat you could see the wide lapel of his double-breasted blue serge suit. I remember, many years later, Momma telling me she paid less than thirty-five dollars for that suit down at Nathan & Sons at 8th & L.

Thomas was wearing a knicker suit. But you probably don't know what knickers look like. They were knee-length trousers that buttoned just below the knee. He also had on his new cap that Aunt Mabel gave him for Christmas. It was like those newsboy caps, kind of flat with a short bill, in the prettiest beige color.

We were lucky, 'cause they opened the doors not long after we got there.

Boy, I'll never forget that rush for seats. Everybody was pushing and jostling, and it wasn't easy for us little ones to stay on our feet and keep together. But we found some good seats, even though they were up in the lower rows of the balcony. Within an hour there was standing room only. It was so crowded that they had to bring in a squad of police to clear the aisles and pas sageways. But everyone was in a good mood and eager to cooperate. Such cheerfulness. It's too bad we don't have more of that now.

After we were seated I spent a long time looking at that enormous space. When it opened, the Memorial Auditorium was one of the finest and largest performance halls on the West Coast. But it meant more than that to us. There was a lot of civic pride involved. I remember Momma telling me about the days before the auditorium, how this one opera singer had come to Sacramento and stormed out of town afterward, claiming that she was never coming back, because there were no adequate facilities here to perform in. Momma used to complain that some acts would not even come here 'cause of that. But the new auditorium changed all that. I remember that some time later another opera star was so pleased with the auditorium, that she asked to be brought back after her performance and be given a tour of the entire facility.

The auditorium meant so much to us then, because all of a sudden we could go see things that before we could only have read about. In fact, the next Monday, Momma took Thomas and me to an afternoon performance of the opera *Hansel and Gretel*. We had never seen an opera before. My, how grand it was to see those beautiful costumes and hear all that pretty singing.

Anyway, once we got in our seats we had nearly an hour and a half wait before the show began. It was my job to take care of Thomas, who began to fidget and get restless. There were no concession stands in those early days, so I had to make up games for us to play; then when I could no longer think up anything else to do, Pop saved the day by producing a big bag of peanuts from his coat pocket. We quietly munched on the peanuts as we listened to the orchestra and choir warm up. Pretty soon I was good and thirsty, but once the program started, I forgot all about it.

The dedication ceremony began promptly at 8 o'clock. Local politicians and dignitaries were gathered in front of the curtain: City Council members, former Council members, representatives of patriotic organizations, the contractors, and others. The stage was all bordered with potted palms and other kinds of plants. It really looked lovely. Then the curtain was raised, and we saw nearly a thousand people on that big stage. There were about four hundred adults in what they called the Municipal Chorus and five hundred school kids in the Children's Chorus. They were all standing on bleachers that stretched from one side of the stage to the other and up and up in row after row. I don't know how they did it. My sister Martha was afraid of heights, and she was in the second row from the top. She said if it wasn't for the excitement of being there, that she would have been totally terrified.

The drums rolled and the flags of the United States, California, and some dozen patriotic and veterans' organizations were marched forward to the front of the room. All of us stood, and the orchestra, chorus, and audience joined together in singing the national anthem. Never in my life had I experienced such a sound. The reverberation of all those voices and instruments seemed to vibrate my very soul. I got a tightness in the back of my throat and my eyes welled with tears. Oh, what a sight and sound!

There were several speeches: Mr. George W. Peltier, President of the Chamber of Commerce, gave some remarks, then Mr. Buron Fitts, the Lieutenant Governor, gave the main address and dedicated the building. He was a past commander of the American Legion and a wounded veteran of the Great War. I find it interesting in reading an article about opening night in my scrapbook that Fitts talked about arousing Americans from a state of indifference, that crime by youth was rising at an alarming rate, and that the cause of most of youth crimes was that of neglected childhood. That message makes me wonder if the "good old days" were really as good as we like to think.

Mrs. Eby, a past State President of War Mothers, talked about the Memorial Chimes and then Mrs.

Rosamond Lamb presented the Keys of the Chimes to the City. Mrs. Georgia Henley, president of the School Women's Club that paid for the flags and flag poles in front of the auditorium, presented them to the City; Mr. H. C. Bottorff, the City Manager, presented the Memorial Auditorium to the City and Mayor A. E. Goddard.

Once all the speeches were over the program moved on to the part we all enjoyed the most—the music. The chorus had been gotten together by Mr. George Sim, the superintendent of recreation, and our symphony director, Mr. Franz Dicks, conducted the orchestra and the choruses.

The musical program opened with the chorus and orchestra doing a series of numbers honoring our war dead. My favorite was "Ring Out, Wild Bells." I can't think right now of all the other pieces they did but I recall the program ended with everybody singing "America," then the orchestra playing Sousa's rousing march, "Liberty Bells."

As we made our way out of the building, I remember that I didn't bother to button up my coat. I was too exhilarated to sleep and too tired to stay awake. I still remember what it was like to feel like a community and how proud I was to be a Sacramentan.....

Opening night at
the Memorial
Auditorium, with
the Municipal
Chorus
on stage.
*California Section,
California
State Library.*

PART I
THE HISTORY

CHAPTER 1

THE STAGE IS SET

In the second decade of the twentieth century, a wave of civic pride swept the country. It was at least partly generated by the patriotism that blossomed during World War I and fueled by the City Beautiful movement that began with the Columbian Exposition of 1893. In passing, it changed the face of American cities, and Sacramento was no exception.

The unbridled physical growth of American towns and cities that had taken place during the second half of the nineteenth century was essentially unplanned. Communities "grew like Topsy," simply building more buildings around their original cores. The lack of overall planning and design consistency raised concerns among architects and planners of the era, and when planning began for the Columbian Exposition of 1893 in Chicago, several of its designers determined that the architectural and landscape or "environmental" design of the exposition buildings should be coordinated and compatible. They chose commonly familiar Classical design themes for all of the buildings, in order to create consistency and a sense of order.

The public responded enthusiastically to the physical elegance and order created by the integration of building design and a landscaped environment, and the concept of urban planning in America was off and running. This movement, which embraced the focus on integrated planning and classical or formalistic design in cities, became known as the City Beautiful movement, and it became a compelling blueprint for community design and construction throughout the country during the early twentieth century.

World War I shifted Americans' naive idea of war from a kind of noble contest between gallant and fair-playing opponents toward harsh reality, and generated a camaraderie derived from group survival. At home, veterans' groups and patriotic societies sprang up around the country. In response, many American cities constructed memorials to the veterans. Often taking the form of an auditorium, the memorials combined the City Beautiful movement, a strong sense of civic pride and identity, and patriotism.

Architect R.H. Hunt reflected on this trend in 1927, when he wrote:

Certain it is that civic pride as expressed through chambers of commerce, boards of trade and a multiplicity of luncheon clubs is now greater than ever, and it is equally certain that more community-wide projects are being proposed and developed than in any period prior to 1917. This existing condition has a bearing on the question of auditoriums, since it is through this type of building more than through any other that this

Masonic Temple, designed by Rudolph Herold in 1920. Postcard, Bonnie Snyder Collection.

civic pride is finding itself made articulate....One of the most frequent of current reasons offered for the erection of auditoriums is that of supplying a memorial to the soldiers and sailors and other participants in the World War...it remains true that no public project is more laudable from a community standpoint than that which serves to unite all elements of the community and thereby to afford opportunity for community assemblies.[1]

These sentiments were not lost on the citizens of Sacramento.

SACRAMENTO COMES OF AGE

Coupled with the civic pride and patriotism in these post-war years was a national spirit filled with an energy, anticipation, and hope that spurred the nation forward into an era of incredible growth, invention and productivity. Most major cities and corporations undertook building programs of unprecedented proportions. This energy and optimism was combined with a growing sense of civic pride and an urge to express it on a grand scale through the building of public buildings, parks, libraries, city halls, schools, banks, hotels, department stores, public works, business buildings, and fraternal lodges.

In this climate, the building of civic auditoriums took on new importance. Cities were anxious to display their pride to visitors, and to benefit from the convention trade. The new prosperity also brought with it an upsurge in cultural endeavors; symphony orchestras and theater groups formed.

Sacramento joined other cities in the country in seeking to capitalize on the promise the national prosperity held. One of the earliest constructions of the City Beautiful movement with its new awareness of urban planning was City Hall, designed by Sacramento architect Rudolph Herold and completed in 1911. Plaza Park, dedicated to the city by John Sutter, was reconfigured to create a formal landscape setting for the symmetry, classical elegance, and rich ornament of City Hall's Beaux Arts design.

Between 1912 and 1928 nearly thirty new building projects were completed in Sacramento. In 1912 well-known Bay Area architect Willis Polk completed the imposing neo-classical National Gold Bank of D.O. Mills and Co. at 7th and I Streets. Herold's Capital National Bank building with its monumental terracotta figures was finished in 1916 and his Masoni

California State
Life Insurance
Company's
building at 926 J
Street, designed
by George Sellon
in 1925. *Postcard,
Bonnie Snyder
Collection.*

Elks Club building,
on J Street, designed
by Starks and
Hemming in 1926.
*Postcard, Bonnie
Snyder Collection.*

Temple with Knights Templar flanking the entry, in 1920. The City Library, designed by Loring Rixford, a San Francisco architect, was built in 1918. The first years of the 1920s also witnessed the completion of the Southern Pacific Depot by Bliss and Faville, and Julia Morgan's Public Market. The Capitol Extension buildings (Library and Courts Building and Office Building #1, now Jesse Unruh/State Treasurer's Office)—almost identical and both designed by Weeks and Day—were completed in 1925 and 1928 respectively. Like the expectations of the city's citizens, some of the buildings, such as the Elks Building by Starks & Hemming, and George Sellon's California Western Life Insurance Building at 926 J Street, reached to the sky.

The list of notable and still familiar central city buildings that appeared between the California Realty Conventions in 1923 and 1928 is astounding. In addition to those listed above were Sutter Hospital, the Senator Theater, the Francesca Apartments, Weinstock Lubin & Co., California Packing Corporation (Del Monte Cannery), and Union Station, among others.

Despite the Great Depression that began in 1929, the building boom in Sacramento appeared to increase in the early 1930s. A 1931 *Sacramento Bee* article announced that eleven large construction projects were slated for 1932, at a cost of $4,019,830, and

Sacramento City Library, 9th and I Streets, designed by Loring Rixford and built in 1918. *Postcard, Bonnie Snyder Collection.*

would employ thousands in a "record-breaking" building program. The $1,000,000 Post Office and Federal Building at 8th and I Streets, three junior high schools, and the Sacramento County Home for the Aged and Indigent were among those projects planned. By 1932, the livestock, poultry barn, and restaurant buildings on the State Fair Grounds had been completed. The work force required to handle all of this construction was prodigious, and with the railroad/railyard workers and the local canneries, created a healthy demand for business. Families had a little left over from the milk money for modest entertainments, and the Sacramento Memorial Auditorium, opening in February 1927, provided a hub of affordable activities for the busy working community, as well as a place of celebration and grandeur for other echelons of Sacramento society.

NURTURING AN IDEA

Sacramento is large enough to support [an auditorium] and is in a position to become a big convention city," said the President of the Sacramento Chamber of Commerce in 1916.[1] Two years later, after many of the approximately four thousand young Sacramentans who had served in the Great War failed to come home with their comrades, the General Secretary of that same body said, "Sacramento needs [an auditorium], and why not erect it and dedicate the building to those who have given their lives for the part they took in liberating the world from tyranny and Prussianism?"[2] These were just two of many similar sentiments exchanged over the decade and a half it took to go from the concept to the reality of Sacramento's Memorial Auditorium.

A civic organization known as the 100,000 Club was the first group to begin promoting the idea of an auditorium. The 100,000 Club began its push in 1910, and merged with the Chamber of Commerce on the understanding that construction would begin by the end of that year. That failed to happen, but the talk and planning continued in the meeting rooms of the civic organizations. While their primary goal was to attract the convention trade to the city, there was no lack of other good reasons for Sacramento to have such a structure. Not only would the auditorium allow Sacramento to compete for the convention trade, but it would build

community spirit, spur growth and trade, and provide a venue for cultural and sports events.

The usual discussions between civic organizations and city government took place over the course of the next several years. The Chamber of Commerce continued to look into the matter, trying among other things to line up potential tenants, while the Sacramento Valley Home Products League refused to endorse the project because the $15,000 that had been allocated was inadequate to erect a building that would be a credit to Sacramento. Three years later, in 1916, with still no action taken by the city, the Retail Merchants Association vowed to take up the matter and raise funds for the building themselves if the city failed to act.

Unfortunately, all the best efforts of the Chamber of Commerce and other organizations were insufficient to move the project forward before Sacramento's and the world's attention focused on the Great War. The discussion and planning ceased while news of destruction in Europe and the deaths of thousands of young American servicemen filled the newpapers.

The ending of the war and the community's eagerness to honor those from the city who had "made the supreme sacrifice" finally propelled the auditorium into reality. Such was the gratitude and patriotic fervor for the role Sacramento's young men played in the victory that the Chamber of

Commerce gave them a "field of gold" welcome home, in which young women scattered poppies along the street ahead of the two thousand soldiers as they marched from the railroad station to the Capitol.

The first proposal to dedicate an auditorium to the veterans came just one week after Armistice Day. Harry S. Maddox, General Secretary of the Chamber of Commerce, publicly stated that he believed an auditorium would be a much more appropriate memorial than a "shaft of granite." He proposed that the names of the fallen heroes be inscribed within the building and that it "perpetually hold within its sacred and honored archives" tablets bearing their names and where they were killed. "I believe," he stated, "a memorial to our boys, commemorating the valor of the dead could also be of service to the living, and I would suggest that the people of this community at once take steps to secure a suitable site for an immense hall which would be erected by public subscription."[3] Maddox's patriotic proposal aroused "a veritable tide of enthusiasm," especially among business, civic, and fraternal organizations. Maddox himself, while believing the announcement might inspire serious thought and consideration of the idea, was not prepared for the overwhelming response. His telephone began ringing as soon as the newspaper hit the street. "I have never seen anything more favorably received, and it seems that the time to build it is right now, while everybody is in that receptive mood. Undoubtedly the proposition has struck a popular chord," Maddox told the Bee.[4] Possibly it was a seed planted by one of the callers, or perhaps an inspiration resulting from the rush of the public's response to his proposal that caused Maddox to elaborate on his ideas by suggesting that a museum be included in the building to display guns, war souvenirs, photographs, and records of achievements of Sacramento soldiers.

Not surprisingly, patriotic organizations such as the American War Mothers Council and the American Legion also pledged their support from the outset. Charles Virden, the President of the Consolidated Chamber of Commerce, addressed the "war mothers" at a ceremony in December 1918, in which the city of Sacramento awarded a medal of honor to the mothers of veterans. Each mother received a ribbon with a star for each of her children who served in the war. It was a highly patriotic event, and the emotional fervor of the occasion was not lost on Virden. He seized the opportunity to state that "the next gift on behalf of a grateful city would be that of a memorial hall in honor of Sacramento's brave soldiers." Elaborating on the proposal, he told the mothers that the building would cost about $150,000, and that the chamber would begin raising the funds after the first of the year. "What we want to know," he continued, "is will all you mothers join in this effort and assist in the campaign?" Following a "roar of applause that fairly shook the building," Virden replied, "Fine, then every one of you will consider yourself a member of this committee."

However, the city administration apparently did not share the chamber's commitment to the project, because three years would pass before the city began to take action. In 1921, City Councilman H. W. Funke brought the matter before the City Council, and an auditorium committee was appointed to look into the project. The committee, headed by Funke, included Mayor Albert Elkus and Councilmen E. S. Brown, E. M. Wilder, and D. D. Sullivan. Both Funke and Wilder were outspoken advocates of project. City Manager Clyde Seavey, confirming the Chamber of Commerce's earlier assertion that Sacramento needed convention space, told the councilmen that, "as the Capital of the State, and because she is the center of the State, Sacramento should have many large conventions and meetings which are not coming here because we have no auditorium for a meeting place." A few weeks later the *Bee* quoted Seavey as he made the official announcement on behalf of the city. Shifting his emphasis somewhat, Seavey remarked, "the need for the auditorium is primarily a need of the Sacramento people themselves, although adequate facilities would undoubtedly attract many conventions here, because of the superior climatic conditions here, the hospitality of the people and the historic traditions that exist here."5

Group after group now began to climb aboard the auditorium bandwagon. The Chamber of Commerce got back into the action when its offer to revive the governor's inaugural ball was refused by Governor-elect Friend W. Richardson because Sacramento had no hall large enough to hold all the invited guests. The chamber, which from the beginning had been a leading force in the drive for an auditorium, viewed Richardson's refusal as just one more reason to renew their efforts.

Mrs. Charles Gilmore, President of the Woman's Council, said that the building of an auditorium was the project in which the Council was most interested since it would allow first-class operas, presentations by world-famous singers, more public meetings of Sacramentans, and more conventions. To drive her point home, she told of a famous singer who had put Sacramento on her concert schedule but canceled when she learned that the only place for her performance was the State Armory.

Mrs. Gilmore's entreaties on behalf of the performing arts community were soon echoed by Edward Pease, a well-known local musical director. In a speech to the Rotary Club, Pease commented on the importance of music in building a strong community spirit, adding that the public concerts, recitals, and community singing that were so successful in other cities required that Sacramento build a municipal auditorium. The following year, as the planning process began, the Woman's Council urged the inclusion of a little theater in the building. A little theater movement had gained support throughout the country, and a member of the Woman's Council, Mrs. W. A. Brandenburger, was a strong advocate. J. M. Henderson, Jr., president of the San Joaquin Bank, joined the chorus for the performing arts when he publicly remarked that Geraldine Farrar, "one of the world's greatest singers," had ended her visit here with a poor impression of Sacramento's performance facilities. He admonished, "that sort of thing will give our city a negative form of advertising, which we should take immediate steps to counteract."[6]

Henderson had also suggested that a spacious auditorium would provide an excellent place for the annual automobile shows put on by the Sacramento auto dealers, implying that their support was to be expected. Shortly thereafter, the Master Builder's Exchange endorsed the auditorium. They went on record as favoring a building that would "reflect the progress and prosperity of Sacramento...."[7] Appropriately, in so doing, the builders articulated another important aspect of the project, that of the building as a symbol. Acting on the previously expressed idea of dedicating the auditorium as a memorial to veterans would, of course, symbolize the city's gratitude to those individuals and families who sacrificed life and loved ones for the good of the country. Here, however, the building was being invested with addi-

tional symbolic qualities. Besides representing the city's prosperity, such a structure would also symbolize Sacramento's civic pride and community spirit, two ideals that were held in high regard in this prosperous post-war era. Likewise, it would affirm the importance of culture to the citizens of the city as it was expressed by those calling for a venue for performing artists. Together with the need to provide size and space sufficient for the identified uses, the idea that the building should symbolize the city to visitors and conventioneers drove the project from this point forward.

The idea of making the building a memorial to veterans that had met with such popularity when it was first mentioned in 1918 now surfaced again with the American Legion requesting the action of the new City Manager, H. C. Bottorff. The matter was settled by a resolution of the City Council introduced by Councilman H. W. Funke. The resolution stated, "It is proper the municipal auditorium, when created, be dedicated as a memorial and tribute to the memory of those of this city who gave their lives in service of our country."[8]

PLANNING IN EARNEST

Although the question of whether to construct an auditorium was no longer in doubt, and support for the building was secured from the major civic organizations, issues regarding the general layout, securing the funding, selecting the site, and selecting an architect remained to be solved.

The auditorium committee sent letters to organizations that had indicated their support for an auditorium, requesting suggestions and ideas concerning the general plan, as well as the types of rooms the building should have. Specifically, the committee wanted to know whether to provide one room for concerts and another for theatrical performances, or if a single room should serve both purposes. The committee also researched some of these questions by getting pictures or sketches of other auditoriums that had been built in recent years around the state.

Locally, they were not at a loss for input. A month later Funke reported that twenty-six organizations supported the project, including the Lion's Club, the Rotary Club, the Elks Lodge, the Kiwanis Club, the Exchange Club, the Knights of Columbus, the Saturday Club, the Church Federation, the Teachers' Association, the Sacramento Builder's Exchange, the Master Builder's Exchange, the Master Plumbers' Association, and the Sacramento Auto Trade Association. Many of the local women's organizations such as the Woman's Council, the Women's Alliance, the Business Women's Club, the Association of University Women, and the Women's Christian Temperance Union, also went on record as favoring an auditorium. At least some of the twenty-six organizations went so far as to appoint their own committees to work with the City Council's auditorium committee in planning for the building.

Although the Chamber of Commerce had estimated the cost of an auditorium at $150,000 in 1918, now City Manager Bottorff had the task of researching the actual cost of the proposed structure. Since the chamber's initial estimate, the scope of the project had grown, and building costs had gone up considerably. By the end of 1921, then-City Manager Seavey's estimate had already risen to $500,000, and he considered putting a bond issue on the ballot in the election scheduled for the year's end. However, lacking sufficient information on which to base a more accurate estimate, and sufficient time to get the information prior to the election, the vote on a bond issue was not taken up at that time.

Bottorff studied the question by examining the experiences of other cities with civic auditoriums. Two nearby cities studied were Stockton and San Jose. Stockton's auditorium had cost $700,000, San Jose's $600,000—a far cry from the $15,000 estimate of 1913 that the Sacramento Valley Home Products League had astutely gauged as too low for a facility that would make Sacramento proud—not to mention competitive. Collaborating with citizens and city officials, Bottorff finally fixed the sum for Sacramento's structure at $750,000. The money was

raised by a bond issue voted on in the election of May 16, 1923, and passed by a healthy majority.

SITE SELECTION

Much more difficult and controversial than securing funds was selecting a site for the structure. A major consideration was the fact that the bond money was specified for the structure and furnishings only, and these items would require all of the available funds. Land had not been included in Bottorff's estimate because it was the city's intention to use land it already owned.

The block between 10th and 11th and I and J streets was the first to be identified as a possibility, as the city had already purchased most of the property as an auditorium site in 1916, when the project was being put forth by the Chamber of Commerce. At that time there had been thoughts of erecting a civic center around Plaza Park, which could include city hall, the city library, and the auditorium. A central fire station had also been considered. One objection to the site was its size.

The city-owned portion of the site was a partial block too small to accommodate what the city was planning. In keeping with the City Beautiful movement that guided many civic projects during this time, the city wanted the building to have a setting of its own with "proper surroundings such as shrubery [sic] and shade trees." This plan, however, required an entire block and purchasing the adjoining buildings was judged to be too expensive. In addition, that block contained the city-owned St. Francis Hotel, which generated revenue. Further, the civic center plans had been spoiled by facing the library on I Street. As early as 1921, former City Manager Seavey had opposed the site as both physically inadequate and symbolically inappropriate.

Three other sites were also given some consideration. The Fox block between 8th and 9th and S and T streets, also owned by the school district, was considered very briefly. The Governor's Mansion at 16th and H, just one block north of the 16th and J site was another briefly-contemplated location. McKinley Park, the remaining site, came under scrutiny about six months later, at the behest of some local women's organizations. The issue they raised was that of parking. While it may have been the earliest local consideration of a problem that would confront Sacramento—and other major cities—time and again in the future, it was ironically appropriate that it should be raised: in 1926, Sacramento led the nation in the number of cars per capita, with one car for every two people in the city.

In opposing the St. Francis Hotel site, Seavey had championed the block between 15th and 16th and I and J, the site on which the building is now located. This was also the location now most favored by Bottorff and the City Council. The property was identified because of its prominent location on J Street—the city's main thoroughfare, its proximity to the downtown business center and hotel district, and its availability to the city. It was also far enough outside of downtown to avoid its competing with either Plaza Park or Capitol Park.

The block was one of the squares deeded to the city as a park by John Sutter and specified for public use. The city had turned the property over to the school district, which had erected the Sacramento Grammar School on the site in 1872. The school, whose name was changed to the Mary J. Watson School in honor of an early principal, was well loved, structurally sound, and architecturally distinguished. It was a three-story brick building with a mansard roof, topped by a belfry. The handsome structure was surrounded by a park-like setting of elms planted by the school district upon the building's completion. By now these were mature, beautiful trees and no doubt an additional attraction of the site. The city's plan was to raze the school and build the auditorium among the grove of elms.

The block's availability rested on a provision in the 1872 ordinance turning the block over to the school district, which stated that the land would revert to the city whenever the board of education ceased using it for a school. Thus the board was requested to relinquish the property. Although Charles Hughes, the school superintendent, agreed to do so, he let it be known that in his opinion the Mary Watson property was not the best choice. The school building was in excellent condition, and he had expected it to serve as a school for another fifty years. The Harkness School at Tenth and P was, he thought, a better selection. That building was too old to be used much longer, and the site, he claimed, was nearer the central business district. "I can't see why we should tear down the Watson building, which has been a monument to civic pride for many years and is still in good condition," he implored.[10] And there were technical complications from his standpoint, as well. Where would the four hundred students at Mary Watson go? There was not room in the old high school at Nineteenth and K. That building, designed for seven hundred students, was already housing more than twice that number. The city had plans for a new high school, but it would not be ready for nearly a year. Furthermore, although the City Council promised to salvage the school materials for the benefit of the school district, the Watson building was worth at least $150,000 as a school and was estimated to cost $400,000 to replace. Nonetheless, Hughes capitulated, and the city reclaimed the site.

The City Council declared that the school district "no longer needs the said square for school purposes and the use of the said site for a municipal auditorium is a matter of greater public necessity and convenience than the use of the same by the school department...." The carefully worded declaration dovetailed perfectly with the 1872 ordinance, precipitating the repeal of the ordinance and the reversion of the land to the city. The issue of completing the high school before moving the students resolved itself by the passage of time. While the city dealt with other legal issues the school board managed to complete the high school.

Mayor Elkus remained steadfast in his insistence that the selected site was the best. He maintained that the parking issue was overstated, since most people going to the auditorium would be staying in hotels, and the 16th and J site was within walking distance of the downtown hotels. Surprisingly, he failed to mention that the location was well served by street-cars, with the numbers 2, 3, and 12 lines passing the site. However, he must not have been listening to all the advocates for the performing arts and cultural events, as it appears he assumed that conventions would be the primary use for the building. In arguing against the McKinley Park site, the mayor also raised the point that the city had spent considerable money improving the parks and would not favor using any of them for the structure. Besides, having already obtained it, what would they do with the 16th and J property if not use it for the auditorium? Since Sutter's deed required that it must be used for public purposes, the only other options would be a public plaza, playground, or school. His argument must have hit home, since the matter of siting the auditorium at McKinley Park was dropped. Although the selection of the site now seemed firm, problems surrounding the site would surface again and again.

CHAPTER 3

GETTING DOWN TO BUSINESS

With the community staunchly behind them and the site obtained, the planners turned their attention to the matter of an architect. In February of 1923, the City Council adopted a resolution that put it on record as favoring a competition under the rules of the American Institute of Architects, for the purpose of selecting an architect. However, no action was taken to follow through on the resolution or to stage the competition.

In September, the *Bee* reminded the council of the idea in an editorial singing the praises of architectural competitions. The writer pointed out that this was the typical method of selecting an architect for major civic projects, and he believed it was the way to get the best possible design, citing the examples of local projects as well as those in other California cities. In Sacramento, competitions had been held for the design of the new City Library on I Street, for Lincoln, Washington, and William Land Schools, and for the Capitol extensions. The article quoted local architect Frederick M. Harrison as saying, "The new civic auditorium...should be in every sense a memorial for the city, a building that will stand for years to come as a building of beauty, utility and a public expression of culture and civic pride." Harrison agreed with the author that a competition was the best way to achieve this, pointing out that a compe-

tition did not preclude a local architect from winning the commission. "There are just as many competent architects here as in any other city..." he stated, adding that whether the winner was local or not, the city would get a wonderful building.[1]

Nonetheless, the city did not hold a competition. Why the idea was abandoned is not indicated by any extant records. However, civic organizations had urged the construction of an auditorium and the city had promised it for so many years, that time must have seemed of the essence at that point. The expenditures of time and money that a competition would have entailed must have been a deterrent.

Instead, late in 1923, the City Council created a Division of Architecture in the Department of Engineering, for the express purpose of facilitating and expediting the design and construction of the auditorium. In January 1924, Councilman Bidwell, who may have been concerned about a possible reaction from the architectural community over the city's change in plans, suggested that the first step towards turning the auditorium project over to the new division should be to rescind Wilder's resolution regarding a competition. Later that month the resolution was rescinded and, although a City Architect had not yet been appointed, the council authorized the City Manager to have the new division develop plans and specifications for the structure.

In February Bottorff announced to the City Council that he had negotiated contracts with two San Francisco architects to assist with the design. G. Albert Lansburgh was hired to serve as Collaborating Architect for a fee of $10,000. Arthur J. Brown, Jr. was retained to serve as Consulting Architect for a fee of $2,500. Further, he recommended to the council that architect James S. Dean, of the local architectural firm of Dean & Dean, be appointed City Architect at a salary of $500 a month. Defending the action, Bottorff explained that the auditorium could be designed more economically by the City Architect and this team than it could under the usual procedure in which the architect received six percent of the project cost. Rough calculations bear out this claim.

Bidwell's concern was not unfounded. Awarding the commission for the auditorium to a team consisting of the newly appointed City Architect and two San Francisco consultants, with no competition or even any consideration of other architects, drew at least one protest. Prominent Sacramento architect Rudolph Herold reminded the council of Section 252 of the city charter, which provided for open competitions for public buildings costing over $2,500. Herold's protest gained him nothing and became a moot point, as he died two years later, nearly a year before the Memorial Auditorium opened in 1927.

Controversial though they may have been, Bottorff's tactics appear to have been well-reasoned. The specialized nature of the project required technical expertise. Lansburgh and Brown were recognized experts in theater design and urban design respectively, and could have handled the job with ease. But the city was anxious to proceed with the project, and the fact that they were located in San Francisco somewhat complicated matters. Thus they were not hired to produce the design, but rather to consult and collaborate. By entrusting the project to Dean, as City Architect, the city effectively absorbed one of the three firms and retained tighter control of the project.

The team was also thoughtfully selected. Both of the San Francisco architects had been trained in Paris at the Ecole des Beaux Arts, the finest and most prestigious architectural academy in the world. Their education at the Ecole focused on monumental buildings in the Beaux Arts style—a style based on Classical architecture that took its name from the school. Lansburgh and Brown were well-equipped for designing civic structures: Lansburgh was nationally recognized as a designer of opulent theaters, and had designed several auditoriums; Brown was known for his advocacy of the City Beautiful movement and for his expertise in urban design and civic buildings. Brown's major projects included the Berkeley City Hall, the Stanford University Library, Coit Tower, and the San Francisco Art Institute. As a team, they were later to gain international recognition for their San Francisco War Memorial Opera House, completed in 1932.

For his part, Dean was also an excellent choice. Dean and his brother Charles, with whom he was in practice, had both worked for the Office of the State Architect for several years, before establishing their own firm, Dean & Dean, Architects, in 1922. The numerous schools and other buildings they designed utilized various historical references and demonstrated the brothers' mastery of the academicism that was the mode of the day.

Within their partnership of Dean & Dean, James was always considered the business head and Charles, the designer. In announcing James Dean's appointment, Bottorff indicated that he would act in a supervising capacity in the auditorium project. What his or the city's intentions were regarding the firm's role in the design of the building is not clear. What is clear, however, is that it played one: Charles Dean and Howard S. Hazen, another designer in the firm, were credited by name as the architectural designers in the building's opening night program. According to Earl Barnett, another of the young designers in the firm who was interviewed by the *Bee* in 1986, both he (Barnett) and Hazen played a definite part in designing the building. Given James Dean's position in the firm, as well as his work for the State Architect, the City Council had clearly selected a

proven administrator for the post. In his later career, Dean continued to capitalize on his administrative abilities and the city continued to benefit from them.

Designs Are Drawn

The collaborating and consulting architects' contracts specified that their work be completed within one year, so they lost no time in preparing the plans. In July, five months after Dean's appointment, the City Council viewed the preliminary plans, and the *Bee* featured a several-column-wide drawing of the main floor on the front page of the paper. Those plans were very close to what we have today. The plan included the main auditorium with the arena seating and the stage. Dean described to the City Council his idea for a tilting arena floor for movable seats, and a movable stage that could be raised or lowered to the level of the arena floor (only the first of these was included in the final design). Dean's presentation to the council was so detailed that he even explained that rubber guards would be placed on the legs of the movable chairs to prevent them from slipping on the tilted floor.

The Mary J. Watson School in the process of being demolished in November 1924, to make room for the Memorial Auditorium. *Eugene Hepting Collection, Sacramento Archives and Museum Collection Center.*

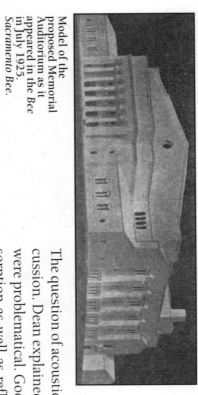

Model of the proposed Memorial Auditorium as it appeared in the *Bee* in July 1925. *Sacramento Bee.*

In addition to the main auditorium space, the design included numerous smaller rooms. Considering the Chamber of Commerce's main intentions for the building, the design team provided space for meeting rooms along the corridors on both sides of the auditorium. To the east and west of the foyer were smaller halls with a capacity of about 350 each.

The City Council, responding to the Woman's Council request, designated the east hall as a little theater and lecture hall. The architect was asked to equip the reception hall—was added to the plans.

The question of acoustics was given considerable discussion. Dean explained that acoustics in a large hall were problematical. Good acoustics depend upon absorption as well as reflection of sound. He recommended that the acoustic design be predicated on the seating capacity of the room as indicated by the plans. That way, when the room was full, the acoustics would be as perfect as could be expected in a space of this size.

The council approved the plans with some minor changes, although many details were yet to be worked out. While Dean had begun work on the exterior design, he said he would not take it much farther until the interior plan was finalized. Dean invited public review of the plans and said he would welcome suggestions from organizations that had ideas for features to be incorporated.

At least one suggestion was not long in coming: the Veterans Affiliated Council noticed that no meeting space had been provided for the veterans. George Klumpp, president of the council, stated that when the bonds were voted, the veterans had understood the building would include such a room. Although this was probably more of an assumption on their part, the room—located between the foyer and the hall as necessary.

While the architects were working on the plans, the city let the contract for the demolition of the old school. Under the terms of the document, signed on November 6, 1924, Acme Lumber Company paid the City of Sacramento $1,260 for removing the school and salvaging the materials. Within ninety days, the Mary J. Watson School existed only in the hearts and memories of its former students.

By the end of the year, the exterior design of the building was completed. Presenting City Council with a model that had been constructed in San Francisco, Dean, Lansburgh, and Brown revealed their plans. "Building will be of Byzantine Architecture" announced the *Bee*.[2] The architects unveiled a scale model of a building that was to be 270 feet long and 214 feet wide with a massive entrance of seven 28-

foot arches on soaring columns. The building would be eighty feet tall at the peak of the roof over the main auditorium. The materials were to be face brick and tile (terra cotta). The best news was that this could all be accomplished within the $750,000 of the bond issue, including the landscaping and interior furnishings. The City Council approved the design and authorized the City Architect to proceed immediately with detailed plans and specifications. Having finally begun the process of producing the long-promised auditorium, the city was now anxious to have it completed as soon as humanly possible.

A Legal Issue Develops

Although the plans for the building were being developed with all possible haste, all was not well with the site selection. Doubts had begun to surface concerning the legality of using the block at 16th and J. City Manager Bottorff felt that two questions needed to be settled: Did the city have the right to build on the property, and could it charge admission? The issue involved the terms of Sutter's deed of the property. The city's dealing with the school board and the careful wording of the council's declaration taking the property back had failed to address Sutter's expressed intentions for the use of the block. Sutter had deeded the property to the city for public use. Would charging admission to events negate that?

The City Attorney, Robert Shinn, felt that there was no problem and had given that opinion in the past. But Councilman Bidwell, also an attorney, was doubtful. The matter went before City Council in January 1924. A quiet title suit was filed by the city, but no one contested it. It came up again in July, when Bidwell said he worried that a suit might be brought against the city after the building was built and an event held where admission was charged. Bottorff suggested that a court test would settle the matter and erase all doubt. Although the floor plans were presented to the council that same evening, Bottorff recommended that someone be found who would take the city to court over the issue before construction was started.

Finally, a local mechanic named H. J. Futterer was prevailed upon to bring suit as a resident and taxpayer. He was represented by Attorney Charles A. Bliss, a former city commissioner. When Bliss informed the City Council that Futterer had agreed to lend his name to this action, Councilman Bidwell suggested that the council give the mechanic a vote of thanks.

So while the architects continued with the drawings, the city prepared its arguments. The case was heard before Superior Court Judge Malcolm C. Glenn, who, after lengthy arguments, rendered the decision that the building could be erected on the site and admis-

James S. Dean, of the local firm of Dean and Dean, was appointed City Architect to oversee the design and construction of the Memorial Auditorium. Gladser Studio, compliments of Grace Taylor Dean.

The Sacramento architectural firm of Charles and James Dean was well established and respected by the time it became involved with the design of the Memorial Auditorium, having begun in private practice in 1922. The Dean brothers originally came to California from Texas, where they had attended Texas Agricultural and Mechanical College (Texas A&M). Their father, R. K. Dean, was an engineer and builder who apparently passed on a strong interest in construction to his two sons. George Sellon, a Sacramento architect who became the first State Architect after the 1906 earthquake and fire in San Francisco, recruited young Charles Dean from the Chicago office of Englehart & Englehart in 1908. Brother James, who attended Massachusetts Institute of Technology after Texas A&M, joined him in 1912 and subsequently served eight years as assistant State Architect to George McDougall.

In 1920, the City of Sacramento launched an ambitious school building program, and in 1922, the brothers left the Office of the State Architect to open their own practice. During the next five years, their firm completed the Fremont, El Dorado, Newton Booth, Franklin, Donner, Bret Harte, Jefferson (now the school district administration offices), East Sacramento, Highland Park, McKinley, and Leland Stanford Schools, and provided additions or alterations to Marshall and Lincoln Schools. They also designed a number of residences in South Curtis Oaks and East Sacramento, the Sutter Lawn and Tennis Club, Sacramento Junior College buildings, the Municipal Filtration Plant, the Sacramento Orphanage and Children's Home, the Golf Club House at William Land Park, and Westminster Church, in

addition to some regional buildings. Charles acted as the principal designer and James as the business or executive partner, until James was appointed City Architect to manage the designing and building of the Memorial Auditorium.

According to architect Nicholas Tomich, who began working with the firm in 1931 at the age of nineteen, Charles was primarily responsible for the choice of design style for the Auditorium, basing it on a smaller building of similar design that he had admired in Washington, D.C. However, while Charles was working for the architectural firm in Chicago in the early 1900s, he certainly must have visited the famous Auditorium Building and its theater, the largest of its kind in the world, that Dankmar Adler and Louis Sullivan completed in 1889. There are certainly similarities in the design image of the proscenium of the Sacramento Auditorium and Adler & Sullivan's Chicago design. While the surface design of the Sacramento building is more Byzantine in reference than the Chicago theater, the successively recessed arches above the stage are similar in form and character.

Charles continued as active manager of the firm while James sold his share of the business to Charles after taking the position of City Architect. James went on to become City Manager, and ultimately, Director of Finance for the State. Charles practiced with Dean and Dean, which had retained the plural name, until his death in 1956. The firm continued under the name of Satterlee and Tomich, completing the design and construction of almost one thousand buildings

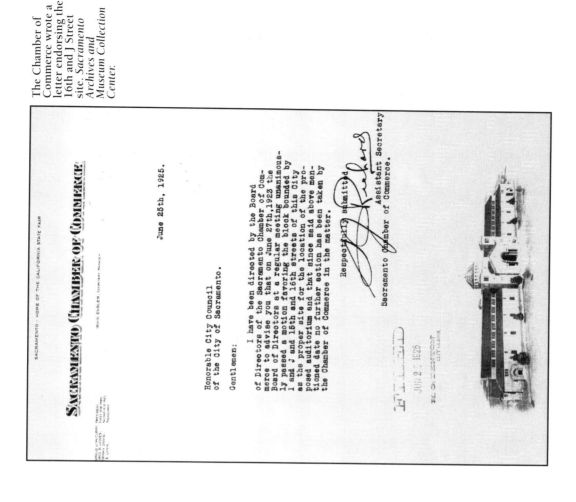

The Chamber of Commerce wrote a letter endorsing the 16th and J Street site. *Sacramento Archives and Museum Collection Center.*

sion could be charged. The decision stated that charging rent and admission were incidental, to be used for the maintenance and upkeep of the building, and did not impair the public nature of the structure. Further, charging fees would not violate Sutter's deed.

A thorough man, City Attorney Shinn supported an appeal to the State Supreme Court to further secure the city's rights and prevent any suits later on. The Supreme Court heard the case in May 1925, and upheld the decision. Bottorff, Bidwell, and the City Council no doubt breathed a collective sigh of relief. The city was now free to use the site and proceed with the construction without fear of objections being raised or law suits filed—or so they thought.

MORE PROBLEMS

Within a month, the Woman's Council, claiming to represent 11,000 affiliated club women in Sacramento, created another headache for the city over the building's location. While the Chamber of Commerce, the Retail Merchants Association, and the Sacramento Realtors Association were writing letters of endorsement for the 16th and J site, some members of the Woman's Council were busy drawing up a petition for an initiative to prevent the city from using the site for the auditorium. The Woman's Council, apparently believing the 16th and J block was too small, wanting to save the site as a public park, and again concerned over parking in the vicinity, proposed that the city exchange the St. Francis Hotel property at 10th and I Streets for the Rink Tract at 31st Street between J and M, or the old Helvetia Cemetery, in the same area. Alternatively, they suggested that the city could sell the hotel and use the proceeds to purchase the substitute property. The main proponents of this plan were Mrs. Hulda McGinn, Mrs. Helen Gilmore, and attorney Arthur E. Miller.

Focusing on the parking issue, the city responded by citing figures compiled by Dean. According to his calculations, within a three-block radius of 15th and 16th and H and J, there were parking spaces for 2,497 automobiles that could carry 7,491 people, more than the seating capacity proposed for the structure. Further, claimed W. L. Elliott, a spokesman in favor of the selected site, conventions would be an important use of the facility, and about seventy-five percent of those attending would be from out of town; thus, he argued, the site needed to be within walking distance of the downtown hotels. Elliott's anger at the women's opposition and potential delay of the project showed when he began his remarks by saying, "I believe that the women are laboring under the delusion that the auditorium is to be built for them alone, but we want this auditorium for something besides musical attractions."[3]

For his part, City Attorney Shinn referred to the city charter to determine whether or not it was legal for the city to sell its real estate. In his opinion, the charter clearly prohibited such an action. Shinn, who had just won for the city the right to erect the auditorium on its selected site by getting a citizen to bring suit, maintained that if the city were to attempt to sell or exchange any of its real property to obtain a substitute location, it would no doubt be sued over it. "Any taxpayer," he said, "would have the right to contest the city's action and I feel certain some interested taxpayer would do so."[4] He contended that the legal ramifications of the issue, if it was pursued, could delay the construction of the building by a year.

Not everyone in the Woman's Council agreed with its pursuit. Indeed, there was some question as to whether or not the park idea was a red herring, although for what remains entirely unclear. Mrs. W. A. Brandenburger was a vocal opponent and took public issue over the Woman's Council supposed representation of all of Sacramento's club women issuing an impassioned statement to the *Bee*: "Are the people of Sacramento again about to be balked in their ardent desire to have the Municipal Auditorium erected without further delay? I believe, if the women of this city understood what mischief is being attempted in their name they would rise up en masse to protect against such ill considered [sic] ac-

Ground Is Broken

While all this sound and fury was going on, a confident Bottorff accepted a bid for excavating and grading the site. As the auditorium would take up considerably more of the site than had the school, the contract included the removal of twenty-seven of the large elms. For the remaining one hundred or so, the contractor, C. Miles, was to construct concrete protectors to prevent damage during the erection of the new building.

With the site cleared and ready, plans for the groundbreaking ceremony got underway. The event, staged by the Chamber of Commerce, was held at 1:30 p.m. on July 16, 1925. The fire department band entertained while the dignitaries and spectators gathered for the festivities. All of the businessmen's organizations attended, some adjourning their luncheons early to march to the scene. Beginning with Mayor Albert Elkus, each member of the City Council turned over a shovelful of dirt with a silver spade. Music during the event was provided by the Reverend Byrl Babcock and by the Rotary octet.

Mayor Elkus addressed the crowd, describing in considerable detail the building planned for the site, and promising completion by September 1 of the following year. The highlight of the ceremony was an address by United States Senator Hiram Johnson.

tion...." She went on to insinuate that the women proposing the change were being duped. "Are not those club women allowing themselves to be used as cats' paws to serve some subtle private interests?" Continuing her attack, she suggested that the women should "learn to appraise political motives, to distinguish propaganda from truth, to stress the application of the principles of common honesty in politics as in business and set an example of higher political idealism in a man's world which still welters in the throes of political disingenuity and deception."[5]

Undaunted by the tirade, Miller, Gilmore, and the Woman's Council committee appeared before City Council in opposition to a delegation of businessmen speaking on behalf of the 16th and J site. A committee spokesman issued a statement saying they had taken the preliminary steps necessary to save the 16th and J block for the people as a park. They requested a show of support by way of signatures on the petition. Issuing their statement on a Friday, they gave the potential signers until the following Tuesday, saying that if they had not gotten five hundred signatures by then, they would not pursue the matter any further. On Tuesday, with only forty-eight signatures on the document, they abandoned their efforts.

Hiram Johnson at the ground-breaking ceremonies, July 1925. *Sacramento Bee.*

Johnson, Sacramento's native son, had attended the Sacramento Grammar/Mary Watson School, as had his wife and his children. He waxed eloquent for the occasion, speaking of his boyhood memories, his pride in his hometown, and his vision for the auditorium.

We dedicate here today a civic improvement not uncommon in the complexity of modern city life. But the structure to be erected here will be more than an evidence of the prosperity and activity of a great people, more than a mere monument to their enterprise. It will represent their vision and within it will abide their spirit. We break ground today for a people's auditorium. It has been decreed by Sacramento's people, conceived and planned, fought for and won by The People themselves, and paid for with The People's money....

The community purposes served by a public auditorium cannot be adequately catalogued. It ministers to our pleasure, instructs and educates, and finally as a public forum aids and conserves citizenship. And among the uses I hope the future holds for this we dedicate to-day is that of free legitimate public expression....

Now we are to have a public auditorium, and it is not too much to hope that when in the future skillful, clever, minister[s] [of] propaganda shall assail or seek to undermine The People's rights, here the voice of righteousness and fair play shall answer in trumpet tones.

I leave you with the vision that is ours of the future of the Sacramento Auditorium: here no money changers shall ever dwell; upon its threshold intolerance shall halt; its walls will re-echo to the strong and powerful no less than to the weak and humble; free speech it shall foster; within it justice and fair play shall abide. It shall be the temple of The People, sacred to the rights of The People.[6]

Johnson completed the day by posing for a photo on a steam shovel and greeting his seventh and eighth grade teacher from the grammar school. With this pomp and circumstance completed, the construction of Memorial Auditorium was officially begun.

CHAPTER 4

BRICKS AND MORTAR

After the groundbreaking, the first moves towards building the auditorium were to order the piles and seek bids for the construction. Apparently eight hundred of the reinforced-concrete piles were ordered prior to selecting a contractor because of the length of time it would take to manufacture them. The piles were completed in early September, and construction bids were opened later that month. Unfortunately, the bids were all too high. Even if the lowest ones had been selected, the project still would have gone over budget. The lowest bid for general contracting was $596,650, leaving only $153,350 for everything else, including the furnishings and stage equipment. The general and electrical contractors' bids were immediately rejected. Those for heating and ventilation and plumbing were held in abeyance. Dean was asked to draw up new specifications in one day's time, and Bottorff requested the city council to readvertise the project.

In the new request for bids, the specifications eliminated the furnishings and equipment, which Bottorff promised to find another way to finance. The other major change was to consider using common brick rather than face brick on the exterior. Bidders were asked to give bids for both types of cladding.

This time Mathews Construction, the previous low bidder, submitted bids of $507,000 using common

brick and $524,000 for the more decorative face brick, a savings of $72,650. The City Council accepted Mathews' bid and decided to use the face brick after all. Bottorff, who had had to explain delay after delay in beginning the construction, must have been ecstatic, declaring that the watchword was "full speed ahead!"[1] While the city was drawing up the contract, Mathews began moving equipment to the site. Construction began in earnest on October 26, with the driving of the concrete piles.

The piles were driven at the rate of one blow every two seconds. The sight of the huge driver, if not the noise it created, drew large crowds to the site. While the spectators may have been fascinated, the neighbors surely tired of the noise. Not only did the pile driver work all day, but the job of cutting the piles to the proper height was continued throughout the night as well. It was mid-December before all the 1,173 piles were in the ground. In January the ninety-two foot, thirty-five ton steel columns supporting the proscenium arch were erected. Construction was progressing on schedule, and Dean announced that the building would be ready by the following November 1.

CORNERSTONE PLACED

With elaborate ceremony, on May 15, 1926, exactly three years after the passing of the bond issue, the

48

cornerstone of the building was laid. Preceding the ceremony, patrols and bands of Sacramento's various lodges and orders paraded from city hall to the auditorium site. Representatives of local patriotic organizations were seated on the platform with city and county officials. The featured speaker of the day was Ezra W. DeCoto of Oakland, grand orator of the California Grand Lodge of Masons. In an impressive ritual, the grand officers of the Masonic Lodge poured corn, oil, and wine, symbols of nourishment, joy and refreshment, over the cornerstone, invoking for the building the good will of the elements. The new mayor, A. E. Goddard, then addressed the assemblage with appropriate sentiments. Interestingly, despite the fact that, given the terms of Sutter's deed, the city's right to use the site for an auditorium had been contested, Goddard referred to Sutter's foresight in donating the land for public use. He ended his remarks by presenting Grand Master Albert E. Boynton with a silver trowel and inviting him to lay the cornerstone. The stone housed a sealed copper box containing current issues of newspapers, city and county reports, plans of the building, names of the city officers, architects and engineers, pictures, chamber of commerce booklets, and other documents. It was placed in the southwest corner of the building.

COMPLETION NEARS

As work progressed on the building, Dean took on the job of designing the memorial to bear the veterans' names. The original plan had been to inscribe the names of all the local men who perished in all of the wars the country had fought, on a plaque or tablet. A partial list of such men had been prepared by the Veterans Affiliated Council and the War Mothers. Fearing that names might inadvertently have been omitted, the list was published in the paper, and the public was asked to review it and notify the city manager of any omissions.

The newspaper followed the building's progress closely, with periodic reports on the percentage of work completed. Although in January, shortly after work had begun, Dean had announced a November 1 completion date, subsequent estimates put it at December 1. By August, completion had slipped to the first of the following year. Nonetheless, reports from the city continued to maintain that the construction was on schedule.

During the spring and early summer of 1926, the site began to look like an erector set. The structural steel members and the 176-foot-long trusses tha[t] were to create the amazing clear span of the arena were put in place. Remarkably, this was all completed without an accident. The erection in July o[f]

By fall the auditorium began to look like a building. *Sacramento Archives and Museum Collection Center.*

the imposing stone columns at the entrance gave the first evidence of the appearance of the exterior. Brick work got underway in August, and Sacramentans began to get a sense of what their much-touted building would look like. The massiveness of the structure must have begun to be apparent as the open steel frame began to be covered in solid material. The brick work was finished by October and the tile roofing begun, signaling the beginning of the interior finishing. The setting of the terra cotta on the exterior was completed in mid-December, the scaffolding pulled down, and the equipment removed. By Christmas the work was being rushed, but the predicted completion date had now slipped to February 1, 1927. Intensive work would be required to meet even that date: much plastering, painting, and other finishing still needed to be done.

With completion of construction nearing, the park superintendent drafted the landscaping plans and put his crew to work. Evergreen shrubbery was selected, with most provided by the city nursery. A local resident gave two camellia bushes as a gift. All planting was to be kept low to emphasize the building itself. The main entrance would be embellished with formal flower beds. Finally, a special lawn mixture was selected that would do well in the shade of the one hundred elms.

THE DECORATIVE TERRA COTTA

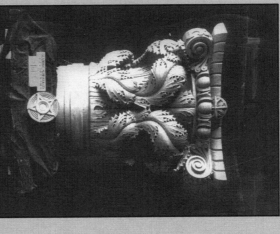

The exterior cladding of the auditorium is face brick and terra cotta. The terra cotta outlines the doors and windows and sets off the building's grand entrance. It was used on many buildings in Sacramento, and most other cities in the country, in the years preceding and following the construction of the auditorium. It was a popular material because it was both durable and decorative. Glazed terra cotta could be made to mimic other materials, such as granite or sandstone, or to create multi-colored decorative elements, such as wreathed medallions.

"Terra cotta" means "baked clay" in Italian. Similar to pottery, terra cotta is produced by packing clay into plaster molds, letting it dry, firing it, then coating it with glaze and re-firing it. The pieces are attached to buildings using a system of hooks and anchors.

The terra cotta used on the Memorial Auditorium was produced by Gladding McBean & Co. in Lincoln, California.

The company began there in 1875 and has been operating continuously ever since. They originally specialized in vitrified sewer tile and still produce enormous quantities of it. In the mid-1880s, they began manufacturing architectural terra cotta. They were the only large architectural terra cotta manufacturer to survive the Depression.

When Dean and Dean, Architects selected terra cotta as a material for the Memorial Auditorium, they began working with Gladding McBean on the color and texture that would be most suitable and most compatible with the brick color. The architects also designed the required pieces and sent drawings to the manufacturer. At the plant in Lincoln, Gladding McBean artists, taking into account the shrinkage of the clay during firing, made models from the drawings. After approval of the models, the company fabricated the plaster molds. Fit is critical when building with terra cotta and a perfect fit is difficult to achieve. After the pieces for the lintels over the side doors were finished, Gladding McBean notified the architects that they had shrunk more than expected. They asked if the door openings could be adjusted from 6'6" to 6'5" to accommodate the terra cotta or if the company needed to re-do the pieces. Dean and Dean changed the doorway dimensions and sent a new set of drawings.

In Sacramento, Gladding McBean terra cotta was also used on the Elks Building, the California State Life Insurance building, the Capitol Extensions, and the Senator Hotel. Other examples of their product can be found in buildings throughout the country. They include such notable structures as the Wrigley Building in Chicago and the War Memorial Opera House in San Francisco.

City council members officially inspected the building on January 31. The opening day, selected for its patriotic associations, was set at February 22—Washington's Birthday. Bottorff, Dean, and Superintendent of Recreation George Sim set to work planning the opening program.

With the opening date set, the rush was on in earnest to finish in time. Workers spent Lincoln's Birthday on the job. The day before the opening, canvas shelters were erected so that the concrete workers and bricklayers could work to complete the sidewalks despite the pouring rain. Carpenters worked through the night putting the finishing touches on the interior. Meanwhile, the symphony and the chorus, preparing for their opening night performances, rehearsed amid the hammer blows.

Finishing touches are being put on the building's interior as painters and plasterers complete the exterior. *California Section, California State Library.*

Sidewalks were being installed while the painters detailed the interior. The building was very accessible to Sacramentans via streetcar with lines passing on both J and L Streets. *California Section, California State Library.*

52

ALL ITS GLORY

The building for which Sacramento had waited so long must have met all the expectations of those who would rush to visit it on opening night. Coupled with the newness of the structure must have been the novelty of its design and features. From the majestic row of columns with their leafy capitals, to the richly detailed interior walls, the massive spaces, and the tilting floor, the Memorial Auditorium was truly a building to behold that rainy evening of February 22, 1927.

Approaching the auditorium, eager visitors found it sitting amid a newly planted lawn dotted with huge old elm trees. Against the building the landscapers had planted junipers, camellias, and ornamental bushes. The imposing structure rose to three stories in height, with towers at the rear and the "flies"—the high open space above the stage from which scenery is raised and lowered—extending another story. Even in the rain, the brick and terra cotta materials

View of the building from the east.
Paula Boghosian.

Sketch of the building by San Francisco architect Francis Todhunter, January 1926.
Sacramento Bee.

An orderly crowd waits in the rain. *Sacramento Bee.*

simultaneously from a wide panorama of historic eras for its inspiration. It was an era that explored the fantasies of the past, mixing them, celebrating them, and creating special episodes that evoked the mystery and excitement of a time gone by—almost like a series of mixed movie sets, inspired by the young film industry. Many Sacramentans were already familiar with the new homes in some of these styles that were beginning to be built in east Sacramento, such as the brick homes that looked like English cottages and the stucco ones that resembled the Spanish colonial homes of early California.

Yet the design elements in the Memorial Auditorium were not those found in other buildings in Sacramento. The auditorium combined Byzantine, Romanesque, and early Renaissance design themes in an eclectic architectural composition best termed as Mediterranean Revival. The building incorporated concepts and details that originated in Italy and the Orient, and then developed in the Mediterranean over a period of more than a thousand years, from the early 4th century to the mid-15th century. However, despite its appearance of antiquity, the building combined a modern structural core of reinforced concrete columns, beams and floors, a roof of steel trusses with wood joists, long-span steel trusses above the ceiling over the main arena area, and interior walls of hollow tile.

While architectural styles have continually been revisited and reinterpreted over time, this period drew

made the auditorium look like it belonged in Sacramento's Mediterranean climate and setting, where there were many other structures made of these materials. The style, however, was unique and defied simple categorization.

Ceiling of entry arcade is decorated with Byzantine designs. *Paula Boghosian.*

The architects had employed a number of standard Byzantine design trademarks: decorative bands of stone (here represented in terra cotta) interspersed in the brickwork; exterior column capitals that appeared incised and drilled rather than chiseled as they would have been in classical times; and a row of arched windows on each side of the building above the upper balcony echoing the row of almost identical windows that encircles the base of the dome in Hagia Sophia, the ultimate example of Byzantine architecture. Five different shades of brick added visual texture to the large expanses of the walls and echoed or enhanced other design features such as the arched windows of the wings and the "blind" rose window centered in the pediment over the columned entry. A special section in the *Bee* the day before the opening quoted City Architect James Dean regarding the design and materials he had selected. He explained, "Wherever the development of civilization has taken place in great river valleys, there has arisen architecture of brick made possible by local alluvial deposits."[1] The brick used in the auditorium had been supplied by the local Cannon & Company and had indeed been made possible by local deposits, but brick had become a popular non-flammable building material in Sacramento after several mid-19th century fires almost destroyed the wood and canvas settlement.

True to the essence of its Byzantine design, the outside of the auditorium reflected some of its interior spaces and uses. The Memorial Hall on the west and the Little Theater on the east flanked the grand entry pavilion. Though not quite identical, these two spaces balanced each other visually and announced, with their different use of plaster and brick, that they were distinct and separate elements from the main portion of the auditorium itself. Cream-colored architectural terra cotta provided a visual design framework and ornamentation that contrasted with the warm shades of the brick, yet tied the elements together.

The main entrance on J Street featured low, wide steps leading to the massive, two-story columns. Five sets of paired doors gave entry to the lofty main lobby. Inside, tall windows in the front wall admitted the blue-gray shimmers of the descending twilight, and arched openings visually connected it to the second-floor balcony corridor. Decorative metal light fixtures hung from the high, handsomely beamed ceiling with its stenciled ornament. Mounted in a place of honor on the north wall of the room above the foyer entry were the names of Sacramento's war dead of the Spanish American War and World War I and standards to hold memorial flags.

The lobby gave access to the two flanking special-use areas. Memorial Hall, a large, windowed, high-

Entry lobby.
Paula Boghosian

ceilinged room with a small complex of mezzanine rooms, had its own double-doored entry off the lobby to the west. The Little Theater was entered through a small foyer, accessing the ticket offices, the stairway to the small balcony of the theater, and the theater itself, through double doors on the east side of the main lobby. It, too, had stenciled ceiling beams and hanging light fixtures in the same style as those in the lobby.

Beyond the lobby was a transverse corridor off of which a doorway flanked by marbled columns and topped with a gilded arch led into the arena. In the arena the vast and sumptuous interior opened away in all directions in an ordered architectural symphony. From the doors at the back wall the stage was 176 feet distant. In a technological achievement for the time, the richly decorated ceiling, nearly 60 feet above the floor, spread over the whole space in a clear span, with no supporting posts or columns to disrupt sight lines. The dress circle on main floor level and the two balcony levels above were arranged in a horseshoe shape around the 118-foot-long, 78-foot-wide main floor. Flights of stairs at the ends of the transverse corridor led to the first balcony level. There,

corridors stretched past checkrooms to the doors leading into the balconies. From the first balcony, steep steps led to the upper balcony.

The proscenium arch framed the 42-foot-deep stage in a 57-foot opening flanked by huge faux-marble columns with gilt capitals. The ornately stenciled proscenium wall glowed with patterned ornament, and the successive proscenium tiers above the stage were moody with symbolic imagery and painted ornament. There were gilded inset panels on the outside surface of the cantilevered balcony wall below the protective metal railing. The decorative main ceiling was framed within a rectangular border that separated it from the functional one above the upper balcony. The frame contained hardware to suspend a curtain and close off the upper balconies and windows from the rest of the auditorium space (although no curtain hung there on opening night). Arched windows high above the main floor on each side of the huge interior space would give a lofty spiritual quality to the space on sunny days, but on opening night showed only the dark night sky. (These windows would later be fitted with wood panels to keep light out during daytime performances.)

Committee rooms opening off of the corridors along the outside walls were configured to open to each other, or to the corridor hallway by means of folding paneled wood doors, (a precursor to the folding wall panels in meeting rooms of many modern hotels that open and close to provide a variety of meeting spaces).

One of the unique features of the building was the ability of the main floor to tilt to combine with or separate from the stage. The main floor, supported on steel trusses, was hinged at the rear and carried on large hydraulic jacks at the front. In its raised position, with wooden panels fitted over the orchestra pit, it became level with the stage and provided one large flat area. For opening night, the floor was lowered so that the stage rose four feet above it, and the movable chairs were arranged for raked, theater-style seating. (Even today the movable floor is a rarity that sets the building apart.)

The footlights at the edge of the stage could be tipped up or laid flat, and sidelights were arranged vertically at the sides of the stage. A large metal control panel with a myriad of knobs, glowing buttons, and switches stood just off stage and controlled all of the house and stage lights. It was "state of the art" in the West. Curtains and backdrops hung high above the stage area in the scenery loft. There were a number of mirrored dressing rooms on either side of the stage and upstairs across the backstage corridors.

Above the vast decorative ceiling was a network of steel framing and rods embedded in a large plaster shell with decorative openings providing ventilation.

A projection room looked down on the arena from behind the balcony at the back of the room. (The signatures of a movie projection crew that presented the first movie in the auditorium still adorn the wall inside.) The basement contained restrooms, fans and boilers, a kitchen, as well as access to the organ's

Interior of auditorium just after opening. *Sacramento Bee.*

The floor is supported on steel trusses (top) and operated by a hydraulic lift (above). *Paula Boghosian.*

58

wind machine, relay system, and console. The latter was accessible to the orchestra pit via narrow stairs on either side of the stage.

Throughout the interior, the auditorium's designers had used gilt, multi-colored paint, subtle glazes, and tinted plaster to evoke a feeling of the past. As in many of the homes in Sacramento, the auditorium's painters had used semi-transparent glazes to soften the spaces and give the surfaces more depth, richness, and translucence. The craftsmen had used a special antiqued treatment on the doors to imitate a dark blue-green copper or bronze metal fin-

ish, and lend a rich and unusual color to the lobby, foyer, and corridors. The rough-finished, terra cotta-color plaster of the corridor walls gave them the character of an old Mission or Mediterranean enclave.

Varied glazes on the walls of the upstairs corridors softened their surfaces and gave them a mystical Mediterranean character, while the richly variegated, glazed earth tones of the half-walls in the arched openings overlooking the foyer below and the variegated finishes and glazes on the ceiling added a translucence and personality to the space.

The design team's understanding of the history of architecture, coupled with their sensitivity towards a style appropriate for the region and an aesthetic of interior finishes, had given Sacramento and its citizens a building worthy of the long wait. The events and patrons soon to come would turn the glow of the interior finishes into the glow of life.

Perforated center
of ceiling coffer
viewed from
above.
Paula Boghosian.

Curtains and
painted back-drops
hang above the
stage (top).
Paula Boghosian.

The control panel
was located stage
right and operated
the lights.
*Courtesy of Vitiello
Associates.*

THE LITTLE THEATER

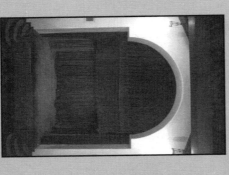

Little theater seats and stage. *Dreyfuss and Blackford, Architects.*

Simultaneous with the opening of the auditorium, Mrs. W. A. Brandenburger, a local leader of the little theater movement, announced the opening of the Little Theater, March 7 and 8, 1927. The play performed on those dates would be "Why Marry," a three-act comedy starring Jean Keller Bouvier and a local cast.

The Little Theater had been included in the auditorium building at Mrs. Brandenburger's (and the Woman's Council's) suggestion, during the planning of the structure in 1923. She presented an impassioned resolution to City Council that explained that the national little theater movement had been establishing itself in the country for the previous ten to fifteen years, and that Sacramento ought to have one. Appealing to the council members' civic pride the resolution stated:

There are many people in Sacramento who [have] long cherished the hope that Sacramento might enjoy the privilege of having a little theater. We have looked with envious eyes at other cities, in no way superior to our own, one after another establishing a little theater, as that movement swept over the country....[1]

Upon the building's opening, Mrs. Brandenburger, a woman of political sensibilities, praised the city for their decision to join the 1,600 other American cities in providing a venue

for "the play spirit and natural craving for expression of the dramatic instinct of the people...." She added that by including the little theater in the auditorium building, Sacramento officials showed "a lively and intelligent apprehension...of the currents and trend of adult education in the field of art and drama."[2]

Also known as "tributary theater" for its contributions to commercial theater, the little theater movement promoted experimental works and gave opportunities to a number of successful actors and playwrights. Eugene O'Neill, Brandenburger pointed out, had begun his career in the little theater movement. Many of the ideas regarding stage and set construction, lighting, and other theater arts that began in the movement were later adopted by commercial theater.

Performing in the Little Theater could be challenging. To cross behind the stage, actors had to exit to the side, open a trap door, descend a ladder, cross under the stage, climb up another ladder and open the other trap door. It was especially difficult to make an entry this way if someone was standing on the trap door.

As well as being used for small dramatic productions by theater and school groups, the Little Theater held lectures and meetings both for the community and for conventions that also used the other portions of the building. The city never really promoted its use separate from the rest of the building, however, and it was generally under-utilized. In the years before the building's 1986 closure, the Little Theater was rented very infrequently.

PRIDE OF ACCOMPLISHMENT

This fashion layout pasted over a photo of the auditorium is evidence of the importance of the new building to the community. *Sacramento Bee.*

Brooding dreams of the Argonauts, who saw that one day a mighty city would rise at the junction where two rivers mingled the snow waters of the Sierras, are represented in this building."[1] So said the *Sacramento Bee* on the day before the auditorium's grand opening. With those lofty words, the writer of the article expressed his belief that the sum of Sacramento's history prior to that date was embodied in the new auditorium.

While that may have overstated the case for most people, the enthusiasm on the part of Sacramento businesses, civic organizations, and citizens who promoted the building of the auditorium certainly did not slacken upon its completion. Nor did the conviction that the building not only symbolized the city's progress but would contribute greatly to its further prosperity. Obviously pleased with the results of their efforts, city officials, businesses, and organizations had high praise and lofty predictions for the magnificent new structure. The building definitely went a long way towards assuaging Sacramento's dogged self-consciousness.

The day before the auditorium opened, the *Bee* ran a ten-page supplement devoted to the new building. City Manager Bottorff spearheaded the praise heaped on the building, saying he felt sure that it would be recognized as one of the most modern such structures on the west coast. Advertisements taken out

by local businesses used exalted language to express their sentiments, ranging from gratitude to those who contributed to the construction, to pride in their city and hope for its future.

From the newly constructed Senator Hotel came, "Sacramentans may well be proud of this beautiful and enduring testimony of their city's progress and social and educational advancement."[2] California State Life Insurance Company, who had just completed their new home office building at 926 J Street, commented, "We share with all Sacramento in Civic Pride upon the completion of the magnificent new Memorial Auditorium."[3] Friend and Terry Lumber Company added their congratulations and praise: "The result of dreams and labor is now before us. Congratulations to our city are now in order. We all unite in enthusiastic commendation of Sacramento's enterprise."[4] The Nonpareil clothing store stated that the completion of the auditorium was the civic development that meant more to Sacramento than any single such event in the history of the city. But Weinstock, Lubin and Company, the city's biggest locally owned department store, outdid all others in its sentiments of civic pride and expectations for the building's contribution to the city. Stating that Sacramento compared well with

larger cities, except for its previous lack of a place for conventions and musical and dramatic presentations, the ad went on to say:

Due to the vision of some of our communal leaders and the energy and skill of our public officials, we now have an establishment of which we well may be proud.

Our Auditorium will serve us in many useful ways. It is a memorial to our patriots. It is a monument dedicated to the Arts. Here, music, poetry, the dance and drama will flourish. It is an encouragement to social contacts, so necessary to the real spiritual growth of any community. It is our Host-house, to which we invite our neighbors from miles around.

Situated upon the site of one of Sacramento's oldest educational institutions, it, too, may carry on the mission of true enlightenment.[5]

Another theme was Sacramento's recent prosperity and growth. Hale Brothers Department Store's ad carried a huge sketch of all the recently constructed new buildings in town to emphasize the growth the city had experienced.

Some of the civic organizations expressed their pride and support by making donations of accouterments for the building. During construction, the Woman's Council had taken the lead in a fund drive to provide the chimes which were mounted on the roof. The chimes would strike every quarter hour and play the "Star Spangled Banner" each evening at 6:00. In addition the Sacramento Teachers' Federation, which may have felt stung by the sacrifice of the Mary Watson School, was nonetheless gracious in the los...

and donated the two flagpoles in front of the building. The Veterans Affiliated Council furnished a huge silk flag for the stage.

The program on opening night reflected both the community and memorial aspects of the building. The program opened with the advancing of the colors by local patriotic organizations. The first half of the program was devoted to city officials and representatives of the civic organizations who all made appropriate speeches and presentations. Lieutenant Governor Buron R. Fitts gave the dedication address. The second half was musical, featuring patriotic and memorial numbers.

What an awe-inspiring sight it must have been when the curtain went up to reveal the stage filled to capacity with the nine hundred-voice Municipal and Children's Choruses, and the seventy-piece symphony orchestra! The orchestra and choruses participated, together or in turn, in performing the various selections. The words to most of the songs were printed in the program so the audience could follow or sing along.

It was such a huge success that there was standing room only, and the police were called in to clear the aisles so the program could begin. Hundreds of others who could not get into the building were forced to wait outside until the program was over and some

of the crowd had dispersed before they could go in to at least get a look at it. It was after midnight before the building was closed. The following evening, with the movable floor back in its flat position, the Odd Fellows hosted the building's first dance.

Bookings Pour In

By the time it opened, the auditorium had already made an impact on the local economy with the number of bookings that had come in. Peter Wilson, the building's superintendent, wrote with obvious pride of the structure and its ability to attract important entertainment to Sacramento, stating:

No one factor contributes more to a city's success and standing than an adequate entertainment structure to properly house great dramatic and musical productions, national and state conventions, amateur pageants and fraternal ceremonials and dances. Such a municipal auditorium is a trademark of progress and prosperity....

With the opening of this splendidly equipped auditorium, Sacramento is put on a par with Chicago, Philadelphia, New York, Boston and other large cities in the entertainment field....Emphatically, it puts Sacramento on the "show map" for all time.[6]

The San Carlo Opera Company brought grand opera to Sacramento for the first time and played to a packed house. *Franz and Otto Dicks Collection, Sacramento Archives and Museum Collection Center.*

Wilson also listed some of the bookings that he had received for the coming months. Although most of them were for conventions, the San Carlo Opera Company was bringing *Aida*, *Hansel and Gretel*, and *Faust* to Sacramento at the end of the month. This would be the first time Sacramentans could attend national opera company productions in their own city. Among other nationally known acts to sign up, humorist and satirist Will Rogers booked the hall for March 15.

The opera series, sponsored by Ben Ali Shrine Patrol and Band, ran Sunday and Monday, February

27 and 28. It was the first non-community event held in the building, and provided a great send off. If ever verification was needed for the claims of the importance of a major arts venue in Sacramento, that first opera series provided it. It attracted the attention of opera fans from miles around. Parties of aficionados came from Yreka, Dunsmuir, Redding, Red Bluff, Chico, Colusa, Marysville, Yuba City, Oroville, Willows, Williams, Woodland, Davis, Vallejo, Rio Vista, Grass Valley, Auburn, Nevada City, Roseville, Lodi, and other nearby cities. Some drove, but other patrons from Stockton and Woodland came by special trains arranged expressly for the purpose.

While enthusiastic opera fans may have been an orderly group, the auditorium superintendent wanted to make sure that his building would be treated with the respect he felt it was due. Wilson's personal pride in the building, and his sense of his duties as steward of such a monument of civic pride, was thus evident in the policies he established for its use. Boxing fans seemed to worry him the most.

Stating his policies publicly, he said:

It shall be my policy to see that decorum prevails at all functions, and that every courtesy is extended to those renting any part of the building. We have decided to permit boxing contests....But I can say most emphatically that no boisterous conduct or vulgar language will be permitted at these shows....Any offenders will be promptly ejected.[7]

In addition to this admonition, Wilson forbade cigar smoking at boxing matches, fearing damage to the beautiful hardwood floor, which needed to be kept smooth for dancing.

Ladies leaving the auditorium after an event in about 1930. *Sacramento Achives and Museum Collection Center.*

Boxing Fans Must Leave Cigars Outside

Wilson Rules Out Smoking Because Of Danger To Floor Contests

Sacramento Bee.

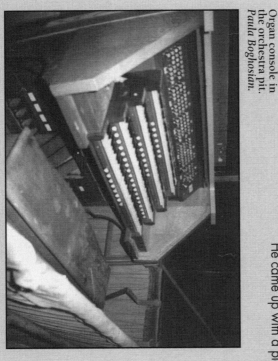
Organ console in the orchestra pit. *Paula Boghosian.*

THE ORGAN

The suggestion that the building be equipped with a pipe organ appears to have first been made in 1922, by bank president J. M. Henderson, Jr. in a speech outlining his several perceived uses for a civic auditorium. A year and a half later his suggestion was echoed by the Woman's Council. Meeting shortly after the appointment of the City Architect, the Woman's Council decided to take steps to ensure that provisions for an organ were included in the plans.

When the city revealed the preliminary design for the building in July 1924, an organ was indeed included, and $30,000 had been budgeted for it. However, after the furnishings and equipment were removed from the original specifications to keep the project within budget, other financing arrangements had to be made. As the plans and construction proceeded, the city manager worked on ideas for alternative financing. He came up with a plan to rent the organ and other building equipment under a lease-purchase arrangement. Chairs, stage equipment, and lighting fixtures were all to be acquired using a lease-purchase plan; the organ was the first to be addressed. After the city council approved the city manager's plan, he advertised for bids based on costs of $20,000 and $25,000. Estey Organ Company, of Brattleboro, Vermont, won the contract, although the price the city ultimately agreed to was $33,750. The organ arrived in three railroad box cars late in January 1927. Assembly and installation be-

gan that same day but had not been completed by the time the building opened.

Organist Wallace Sabin, of San Francisco, played the dedication concert on March 30, 1927. Sabin had been the city's acoustics and organ consultant for the project. He was joined in the concert by a group of "radio artists," including Howard Mulholland, an announcer and singer, the Arion Trio, and Virginia Treadwell of San Francisco's KGO. Three additional organ programs were scheduled for April and May. They, too, featured singers and other musicians in addition to the organ.

How the Organ Works

Any large pipe organ consists of several types of organs, or divisions, as they are called. Each division is made up of groups of pipes contained in "ranks" or "stops" of about seventy-three pipes each. Each division is controlled from a separate keyboard or "manual" of sixty-one keys.

The individual divisions included in a combination depends on the effect desired and the use to which the instrument will be put. The auditorium's organ can best be described as a concert, or orchestral/classical style organ, as opposed to a theater organ. It was custom designed for the Memorial Auditorium by the Estey Company engineers. The combination was designed to create an instrument that could be used for playing solo concerts, accompanying the symphony, and providing music for functions such as graduations and religious ceremonies. It gives a broad sound with generous scaling appropriate for filling a huge space, and is best for playing Romantic or Victorian music; Bach does not sound quite right

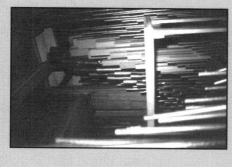

Some of the pipes that make up the huge organ. *Paula Boghosian.*

Relays connect the console to the pipes sending signals that operate the organ. *Paula Boghosian.*

on it. This type of instrument was in vogue at the time the auditorium organ was built. Interestingly, this style is now experiencing renewed popularity.

The organ in the auditorium consists of one pedal division and four manual divisions. The manual divisions are made up of a great organ, a choir organ, a swell organ, and a solo organ. The five total divisions contain 3,555 pipes in forty-eight ranks. The pipes vary in size from huge wooden pipes, the largest of which is sixteen feet long, to tiny pipes about the size of a pencil.

The pipes are housed in chambers on either side of the stage. The solo and swell organs are on stage right (as viewed by the performers), and the great, choir, and pedal organs are on stage left. The proscenium wall is pierced to allow for the flow of sound into the auditorium. Louvers between the pipes and the pierced openings of the choir, swell, and solo organs may be adjusted to eight positions by the "expression" pedal at the console. The con-sole, the unit from which the organ is played, moves vertically seven feet from its housing in the basement to the center of the orchestra pit on a hydraulically operated shaft.

The console was state of the art when it was built. A specially of the Estey Company, it was known as a "cash register" style console, because the stop controls are buttons displayed in groups arranged like keys on a cash register. When the stop buttons are pushed they light up. Unfortunately, this was some-times a problem for the organist, because the lights were hard to see when spotlights from above shined on them. The Estey cash register console was unique in the organ building indus-

try, and the one in the auditorium may be one of the last left in the country that is still playable

Between the pipes and the console is a complex system of operation. The wind that creates the sound in each pipe is generated by a turbine blower and carried through steel ducts to the various sections of the organ. Within each division the wind is routed, via regulators, into the valve boxes or "windchests" which hold the pipes, each with its own pneu-matic valve. Relays send on and off impulses to the various divisions, ranks, and individual pipes as the organist depresses the buttons and keys on the console.

The organ has been unused since 1980, and damage has occurred to it in the intervening years, but in 1990 a group of organ enthusiasts powered up the blower and found the in-strument to be playable. Scott Nelson, an organ restorer, conducted a thorough assessment of its overall condition. There were various problems, one being a seriously leaking windline where a circus elephant, housed in the basement, stuck its tusk through a large duct. There are also some missing pipes and deteriorated materials, but it is repairable. The console also needs consider-able restoration on both the inside and the out-side. The case needs refinishing, but is intact ex-cept for the top which has been replaced by formica. The original top was broken during a rock concert when a guitarist, intending to jump onto it, instead jumped through it.

The auditorium was the center of the whole
cultural life of Sacramento.

Hulda Stone

PART II
THE MEMORIES

THE CHIMES

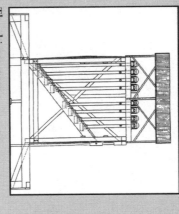

The chimes were housed on the roof of the auditorium and operated by a timer mechanism in the basement.

In 1923, the Sacramento Chapter of the American War Mothers suggested to the Chamber of Commerce that a set of chimes be installed in the proposed auditorium. They planned for the chimes to play the Star Spangled Banner at six o'clock every evening, feeling this would be fitting memorial to their fallen sons. They intended to raise the money for the chimes by soliciting one dollar from each adult, and ten cents from each child in the city. The Chamber of Commerce voted to support the project, and chimes were included in the building's plans when first announced by Dean in 1924.

The Sacramento War Mothers began fund-raising activities in the spring of 1926 and enlisted the support of other civic and patriotic groups. The American Legion promised to help by following up on the War Mothers' solicitations in "any case where a flat refusal may be made without apparent good cause." The Sacramento Church Federation also joined the effort, voting to carry the message to their membership in the next Sunday's service, using ex-servicemen to make the appeal, when possible. The County Sheriff offered assistance by assigning a deputy to escort a committee through some of the areas.

The county Board of Supervisors and the City Council both appropriated funds to help with the project. In September the War Mothers ordered a set of chimes from the Deagan Company, and the city agreed to pay the shipping charges. Mrs. Rosamond Lamb, of the Sacramento War Mothers, presented Mayor Goddard with the key to the chimes during the opening ceremony for the building.

The chimes consisted of sixteen brass tubes ranging in size from five feet long and one and one half inches in diameter to

fifteen feet long and five inches in diameter. They were arranged in two parallel rows in a roofed wooden frame erected on top of the building.

The Memorial Auditorium chimes not only played the national anthem at six every evening, but struck the Westminster peal and the time at fifteen-minute intervals. They were operated by a mechanism triggered by a big black-framed, white-faced clock. Much like a huge, old-fashioned music box, a steel drum was fitted with pegs arranged to strike metal fingers that, in turn, activated electrical relays. The relays caused plungers to come out of their steel housings and strike the top of each tube in a succession that produced the tones and the anthem. Other tunes could be played using a keyboard attached to the organ console.

During World War II, when the country went on twenty-four hour work days, Sacramento night-shift workers requested that the chimes be silenced. The workers, who had to sleep during the day, were kept awake by the quarter-hour sounding of the chimes. The chimes ceased to play about that time, although the reason may have been a broken mechanism that was not fixed, due to wartime shortages. Nonetheless, others, who had complained to the auditorium staff from time to time that the time signals were not in "sync" with their watches, may also have been pleased by the cessation.

The chimes were restarted in January 1946 but stopped again sometime later for reasons unknown–although rumor has it that a governor, living the the Governor's Mansion just behind the auditorium, got tired of hearing them. In time, lack of maintenance took its toll. They were removed from the building in 1979, and are presently housed at the Sacramento Archives and Museum Collection Center.

CHAPTER 7

Decade One: 1927 - 1937
Years of Newness and Novelty

15th amd J Streets, looking west toward downtown, at the end of the auditorium's first decade. *Callifornia Section, California State Library.*

The auditorium's first decade witnessed the new facility's growing pains. Directions were set, then shifted; community feelings aired, and policies adjusted. For the country the decade began as a period of euphoria, with the post-war prosperity continuing to bring technological advances. Charles Lindbergh became a new American hero by completing his solo flight across the Atlantic on May 21, 1927. The city shared very directly in the excitement of Lindbergh's triumph as he had landed at Mather Field in February 1927, at about the time of the building's opening. For Sacramento, it was also a period of prosperity, as the auditorium began to fulfill its promise, and building in the city continued apace for several years. The same decade soon turned into one of despair, however, as the effects of the stock market crash of 1929 gripped the country, and of sorrow, when Lindbergh's infant son was kidnapped and murdered in 1932. The novelty of the auditorium and of the opportunities it afforded Sacramento and its citizens, however, lasted for the best part of the decade. It was reflected in both the entertainment and the economic sections of the newspaper, which gave up considerable column space to nearly anything and everything that involved the new structure.

While the auditorium was in part a product of the city's prosperity in the years following World War I, it was also a factor in its continuing growth for the next five years. As better roads throughout the state and the advent of commercial air travel throughout the country enabled tourists to visit the city, the au-

The California Music Teachers' Association's 19th annual convention held at the auditorium in 1929. *California Section, California State Library.*

ditorium was always high on the list of its attractions. Improved transportation also enhanced the chamber of commerce's ability to draw convention-eers to the auditorium. In 1928, when the California Real Estate Association held its annual convention in the city, the real estate agents were surprised at the changes over the five-year period since their last meeting in Sacramento. The auditorium in which they met was one of those changes, but a dozen more buildings had been erected in the year since its opening. And the growth continued: Within the next several years, additional major buildings would grace the skyline, including the Library and Courts Building at 10th and Capitol and the post office and federal building at 9th and I. In addition, the chamber of commerce began planning for the establishment of the four-year California State College in Sacramento.

THE FIRST YEAR

The auditorium spent its first year living up to its expectations very well, indeed. One of the earliest signs of the hoped-for national publicity for the city came in mid-year, when the auditorium was featured in the *American City Magazine*, complete with a photo. Whether from that source or others, the building attracted a lot of attention. Superintendent Wilson reported that an average of seventy-five people a day were visiting it. "We have had people from all over the country who say they have read about the auditorium and want to see it," he told the *Bee*. The interested visitors included architects and engineers who came to examine some of its special features and to gather ideas for auditorium projects in which they were involved.

While the attention the building got from the curious and interested brought fame to Sacramento, the real test was whether it could attract the number o people necessary to bring added prosperity to the city. The city's operating philosophy was that the auditorium was a community facility, not a profit-making venture, but the events that took place in the auditorium would bring the visitors who would put their dollars into the economy and stimulate business. In other words, the auditorium was not to be money *making*, but money *generating*.

In fact, the sightseers were *not* the only visitors. If its early months were to be any indication, the money-generating philosophy would prove itself. The bookings rolled in and kept the building busy. The bookings varied among conventions, community gatherings, sports (boxing and wrestling), and cultural events—mostly opera. Westminster Presbyterian Church reserved the building for eighteen consecutive Sundays while its new church was being constructed.

Meanwhile, the city was adding up the bills for the equipment and furnishings. By May the total was about $140,000 over the amount of the bond issue. The excess had to be financed from the city's current budget. Although those expenses put red ink on the balance sheet, operating expenses were well covered by the receipts, and the building showed a profit (not considering payments on the incurred debts) for its first six months of operation. By far the biggest source of receipts was rent, which generated $13,563.00—quite a substantial amount considering the rate struc-

ture for the building. The rental fees depended upon the type of event, whether it was held during the daytime or night, whether or not admission was to be charged, and what portions of the building were to be used; they ranged from $75 to $250.

The year 1927 ended with the auditorium's dance card still filled. In fact, dances made up a healthy portion of the schedule, with such organizations as the Musician's Union, the Fire Department Relief Association, the Benevolent Order of Elks, and the State Employees Association all holding their annual balls there. While most of the dances were in the main auditorium, the International Order of Odd Fellows (I.O.O.F.) Colored Club held their annual ball in Memorial Hall. The "hi jinks" New Year's Eve ball of the trades and labor unions closed the calendar. The major cultural events that highlighted the end of the first year were: a lecture by Prince William of Sweden; a concert by the Florentine Polyphonic Choir of Florence, Italy; the opening of the Sacramento Symphony's season; and after the first of 1928, the Notre Dame Glee Club.

The only real complaint about the building must have been the comfort of the movable seats. Those originally supplied did not meet the specifications and were replaced by the manufacturer. However, Bottorff also promised cushions for all of the chairs on the main floor, when funds allowed.

GROWING PAINS

Within a year and eight months after the grand opening, a dispute arose over the rates and rental policy established by the city manager and the building superintendent. The controversy was apparently set in motion by parties who felt that they should get rate reductions, and who brought the City Council into the fray for their own purposes. Although Peter Wilson was named the auditorium's superintendent and set the use policies and rates just prior to its opening, the city, responding to complaints from musical, dramatic, business, and religious organizations regarding the high cost of renting the structure, decided that the guiding philosophy for use of the building needed to be publicly reviewed. Local organizations felt that their uses should have precedence over commercial shows. About forty people appeared at a city council meeting to offer their opinions on the matter.

One of the people who addressed the council that evening was George Peltier, president of the chamber of commerce. As much as the chamber of commerce had promoted the building of the auditorium, Peltier, himself a theater owner, argued that the building should never be used for theatricals or motion pictures that would put it in direct competition with the local theaters. The suggestion got an immediate response—a *Bee* editorial called it "nonsensical," adding:

The Memorial Auditorium is the property of the sovereign People of Sacramento. They built it for a specific purpose—that of having a splendid edifice in which these entertainments could be given and in which a vast concourse could appreciate them.

If the citizens who voted this tax upon themselves had any idea that any such restriction was to be placed upon the use of their property they never would have voted for the bond.[1]

The editorial writer also felt that there should be no rate adjustments. He argued that the auditorium should charge what was necessary to pay its expenses, suggesting that if it began to show a loss, "the very people now asking for such reduction would be the very first to rise up and point to the deficit as an unanswerable argument of the inefficiency and idiocy of municipal ownership!"

An auditorium committee was appointed by the mayor to review the rate structure and find ways to increase the building's use. In August 1929, the committee's report came before the council for final approval. Although a motion was made to accept it, Councilman R. E. Conley read a resolution rejecting the report and revising the rates in various ways. Although the mayor reminded the council that it was not within their purview to interfere in the building's administration, Conley's resolution passed. The win-

ners in the skirmish were events that charged no admission: local musical and literary clubs and their like; athletic exhibitions; and public dances. The theater owners, whom Peltier had represented, were also big winners; a heavy increase was imposed on professional theatricals, concerts, operas, and motion pictures when admission was charged. Interestingly, the most significant adjustment was raising the rent for events on New Year's Eve. At $400, New Year's Eve users would pay the highest rent charged.

It was the latter adjustment that raised the first hue and cry. A local orchestra manager, who had signed an agreement to rent the auditorium for a New Year's Eve dance insisted that he be given a permit at the old rate. During the City Council meeting in which the matter came up, "Enough speeches to fill one issue of the Congressional Record were made before the council decided to grant the permit." Veering from the subject at hand, many of the speeches and exchanges focused on appropriate uses for the public auditorium. Although many organizations had held dances there, Mayor Martin Welsh announced that he felt it "a desecration of the building to use it for public dance." After Councilman Maddox intimated that he had seen some shows there that were so risqué as to make a public dance "look like a parsons' picnic by comparison," the mayor retrenched and said his objection was not to dances being held in the building but to private individuals making

money from them. The mayor's opinion notwithstanding, the orchestra manager got his reduced-rent permit.

This was not the first time that public dance events at the auditorium were the subject of concern, however. The City Council expressed considerable anxiety when the American Legion requested a permit to hold a marathon dance in the building in July of 1929. A marathon staged in Fresno by the same promoters had aroused a public outcry from organizations there, and the council worried that such an event would elicit the same response from Sacramento women's and religious groups. But the marathon was an economic plum, as it would use the building twenty-four hours a day for at least three weeks during a period when nothing else was scheduled, so in the end the council granted the permit.

If the appropriate use of the auditorium was a recurring topic, so was the issue of rent—especially reduced or waived rates—perhaps because the City Council was the arbiter in such matters. In December 1930, the manager of the Fox Senator Theater requested free use of the building for a Mickey Mouse Club show co-sponsored by the *Sac-*

ramento Union. His request was denied because, although the show was free, his was a commercial enterprise. A few months later a councilman, who was also a member of the Fraternal Order of Eagles, requested half rental for an Eagles function. Even though several other council members were Eagles, he was soundly defeated.

While the chamber of commerce's fifteen-year drive for a municipal auditorium had been for economic purposes, the city's philosophy established during the years of planning remained unaltered: The auditorium was a public building for the use of the community. The auditorium's presence in the city would bring cultural events to the city that had not been available before; it would bring revenue to local businesses by luring conventioneers; but first and foremost, the building would be Sacramento's gathering place. The revised rental structure and the City Council's decisions in cases of dispute upheld this philosophy.

Later in the decade another minor dispute surrounded the issue of beer. In 1919, while Sacramento was busy enjoying the post-war building boom and beginning to plan its municipal auditorium, Washington had passed the Volstead Act, prohibiting the sale of alcoholic beverages. In 1933, when the act was repealed, the City Council had to grapple with the issue of whether or not to sell beer in the build-

ing it had worked so hard to get during the "dry" years. In spite of a protest by the Musician's Union, which was about to hold a ball in the building, the council voted to ban the sale of beer in the auditorium, on the grounds that children attended events there and it was not a proper place to sell alcoholic drinks. A week later, however, the ban was modified to allow private parties of adults only to serve the beverage.

The decision was announced by the City Manager, who at this time was none other than the former City Architect and auditorium designer, James S. Dean. Dean had resigned as City Architect in 1928. Then in 1930, during another contentious City Council meeting, he was elected City Manager, replacing H. A. Kluegel. "Ousting" may be a more accurate term, however, as Kluegel was apparently unpopular in some circles and was removed from his position by the seven to two vote electing Dean.

The move to replace Kluegel was predicted by the *Bee* prior to a caucus in which the plan was hatched. When the resolution was brought up at the council meeting, Kluegel, who had refused a request to resign, left the room amid audience applause. The two dissenting councilmen protested the vote, saying that Kluegel had not been given a chance and other applicants had not been properly considered. One shouted: "You can't do that, Mr. Mayor. You didn'

Opera fans line up for performance by the Chicago Civic Opera in 1928. The conductor and musical director in the inset were given standing ovations. *Sacramento Bee.*

give me a chance. You dropped your gavel too soon. You're not fair."[2] Recriminations and defense of the ousted manager followed, and Mayor Bidwell finally agreed to reconsider the matter at the next meeting. With a sound majority in favor of Dean's election, however, the reconsideration changed nothing.

During his long term as City Manager, Dean had to make many other decisions regarding "his" building. Most were minor, but one near the end of the building's first decade is worth noting as it bore directly on the building's design. In 1936, after a dramatic performance brought criticism of the building's acoustics to a head, Dean banned the use of the main auditorium for such events, saying, "The production of dramatic shows in the auditorium is unfair to the public and the players and brings unwarranted criticism upon the city." Dean said that the booking agents had been asked not to book drama into the auditorium, but had not heeded the request—hence the ban. In a slightly defensive tone, he explained that the space was not designed for such productions, but for events such as concerts in which the larger house maximized the acoustical qualities. At the same time, he voiced his opposition to the construction of a municipal theater, suggesting, no doubt somewhat tongue-in-cheek, that it would be cheaper for the city to pay the costs of local enthusiasts' trips to San Francisco to see plays, than to erect a theater in Sacramento!

Dean made a far less controversial decision when he allowed the No. 61 American Legion Post to place their two cannons on the auditorium lawn flanking the main entrance. The cannons had been at the entrance to the post's 7th and I Street building, until a remodeling left no room for them. The cannons remained in front of the auditorium for several years. One was stolen, the other moved to William Land Park, then to a cemetery.

Sacramento Room, Sacramento Public Library.

OPERAS TO PRIZE FIGHTS

While theater had thrived in Sacramento for many years and concerts were plentiful, Sacramentans were starving for other cultural opportunities—especially grand opera. The first cultural event at the auditorium was one of a series of operas which Superior California opera lovers did not have to go to San Francisco to hear. Opera was one of the most popular affairs held in the auditorium during these years. It was one of those types of functions for which the building was made to order. In 1928 the Chicago Civic Opera Company was lured to the city by the magnificent new venue. Sacramento was one of just nineteen cities on their tour schedule. The company performed *Cavalleria Rusticana* and *I Pagliacci*. The producers and singers were not disappointed. On the contrary, they heaped praise on the building. The famous Mary Garden, their prima donna, was thrilled by the acoustics which she could tell carried her voice very well. She also loved the amenities in the building, declaring it one of the finest auditoriums in which she had ever sung. A representative of the opera company's administration was similarly impressed. He stressed that but for the auditorium, his company would not be able to come to Sacramento, adding:

Sacramento is to be congratulated upon having a building so impressive and beautiful on the outside and so completely and adequately designed and equipped inside....

The great stage, equipped with the very latest devices, and the spacious auditorium giving complete visibility from every seat make the auditorium one of which the people of Sacramento can be justly proud.[3]

The company returned the following year to stage *Thais*. With the previous year's performances still vivid in his memory, State Senator Inman proposed that no meetings be scheduled in the legislature on the night of the performance, stating, "It seems fitting that the legislators be released from their duties in order to avail themselves of this rare musical opportunity."[4] Such occasions made the auditorium at least as important to culture-seekers in the other cities and towns of northern California as to Sacramentans. Anticipating her trip to Sacramento to see *Thais*, a grateful Chico woman declared, "To [be able to see] grand opera within a hundred miles of one's home is an opportunity too good to lose."[5]

The comic opera *Mikado*, and the musical *Desert Song* also played at the auditorium during its first decade. Symphony and organ concerts and famous singers on tour, such as Marian Anderson who appeared

---

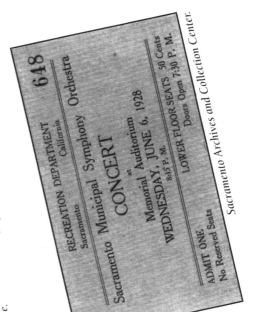

Governor James Rolph, Jr. and Lieutenant Governor Frank Merriam, as pictured in the program from Rolph's 1933 Inaugural Ball at the auditorium. Merriam succeeded Rolph as Governor in 1935. *Courtesy of Matt Lease.*

Sacramento Archives and Collection Center.

there in February of 1937, rounded out the musical schedule. Sacramento High School used the building for proms, graduations, plays, and pageants. Westminster Presbyterian Church held their huge Easter service in the auditorium, and the First Church of Christ also used it for large gatherings. Local clubs, organizations, and businesses held various events, including balls, lectures, and other entertainments. Some of the lectures were held in the Little Theater. One of the more unusual organizations to put on a play in the building was the dredge engineers. For their annual balls, the electrical workers used their skills to flood the building with light, inside and out, in electrical spectaculars. In 1930, four thousand people attended the ball, which was written up in national electrical magazines. The following year, Governor Rolph staged the first of many inaugural balls to be held in the auditorium. Governor Merriam followed suit in 1935.

Big names in other areas were also attracted to Sacramento by the new venue. Will Rogers appeared at least twice in the decade, once three weeks after the building opened, and again in December 1928. Major Bowes Amateur Hour came to the auditorium late in December of 1935. Ted Mack, the band leader, who later took over the program, was the master of ceremonies. About three thousand Sacramentans attended despite the heavy rain that fell that evening.

Boxing matches, or "fights," were held on a regular basis throughout most of the decades, as were wrestling matches. Tennis and basketball tournaments also made their debut at the auditorium during these first ten years. Although no actual game was played there, even football fans went to the auditorium to indulge their love of the sport, when the Sacramento Junior College football coach held a workshop in 1930. The coach explained formations and plays while the team demonstrated them on the arena floor.

Sacramento High School also held a football rally there in 1933 to boost their game against Stockton High School. In these days of a single high school and great community participation in such events, the rally began with a parade of thirty-three floats. City Manager Dean opened the festivities in the auditorium with the first speech. Following several other speakers were performances

One of the first boxing matches held in the auditorium. *Sacramento Room, Sacramento Public Library.*

by a fifty-piece military band as well as the various high school bands and glee clubs.

In this day of computers in every home, unless you are old enough to remember, it may be difficult to imagine a typing contest filling the Memorial Auditorium. However, in 1928 Sacramento made history by hosting the first such competition to be held outside of New York. Sacramento's event was one of the features of the twenty-third annual international typewriting contest. State champions from every state and from some provinces of Canada—approximately one hundred in all—came to compete.

A dance marathon, the cause of the local controversy already discussed, was another event that was linked to this period. Others that were less fun came about because of the Depression. Two such events took place in January 1933. In the first of these, hunger marchers were allowed free use of the auditorium for an "unemployed convention." City Manager Dean granted them permission, but denied them the cots and bedding they also requested. Dean stated that they should have a "designated place to go" where they could "blow off steam," rather than having to wander around. Steam may also have arisen from the convention of three thousand depositors who lost money when the California National Bank and the California Trust and Savings Bank suspended opera

y. m. l.   Seventh Annual   y. L. l.

KOSTUME KARNIVAL

JUDGES

MR. D. C. LEWIS
HALE'S—Decorator

MISS MERNA DE PHILLIPS
Buyer, Bon Marche

DR. J. D. COYLE

MISS UNA BELL
Bon Marche Dress Department

MR. GERALD DESMOND
Attorney

MR. ROY CLAIRE
Convention Bureau
Chamber of Commerce

MR. H. J. TREGELLAS
Tregellas-Mansfield Co.

TUESDAY EVENING
October Thirty-first
1 9 3 3

The Kostume Karnival was an annual pageant and dance held from the late 1920s to the mid-1930s by the Young Mens' Institute. Pictured is one with a Southern theme. *Courtesy of Janet Galante.*

tions. The meeting had been scheduled for the Travelers Hotel but was changed to the auditorium when so many people turned out. At the convention, the depositors formed the Depositors Protective Association to represent their interests and help them regain their lost funds.

One of the more entertaining events that began in the early years and continued throughout the first decade was the "Kostume Karnival" held each Halloween. Put on by the Young Men's Institute, the Karnival featured a pageant followed by a dance. The participants and audience came in costumes inspired by the theme set in the pageant. Photos of the pageant were displayed in the auditorium lobby for many years afterwards.

A Spring Festival held in 1931 may have been a harbinger of the Camellia Festival that would begin ten years later. The Spring Festival featured King Orange and Queen Camellia and their court, an exposition of citrus, flowers and agricultural products, dancing, a fashion show, vaudeville acts, performances by radio artists, various pageants, and the obligatory sprinkling of speeches. A community event that reached beyond

Auto Show committee of the Sacramento Motor Car Dealers Association in February 1932. *Sacramento Bee.*

the boundaries of Sacramento, the festival included the participation of numerous local groups and drew agricultural entrants from several other states.

At the close of the auditorium's first decade, building supervisor Peter Wilson announced that it would close for the month of July 1937 for repairs and acoustical improvements. Wrestling matches scheduled for the month would be allowed to continue while the work was undertaken, but Wilson requested the indulgence of the fans during that period. Perhaps by way of encouraging their patience he assured them that when the improvements were completed, "The wrestling patrons will be able to hear the grunts and groans of the wrestlers in the most remote recesses of the auditorium...." The work included installing plaster grills on the main ceiling covering them with expanded mica, and putting an acoustical plaster treatment on the ceiling over the upper balconies.

The Messiah staged by the Recreation Department in March 1928. California Section, California State Library.

Sacramento's Melting Pot

Many ethnic groups attended the annual folk dances festivals, though not everyone came to see the dancing. The young man on the right of the balcony is clearly more interested in the popcorn box he dropped (left).

School Superintendent Melvyn Lawson and his wife attending a concert (below left). *Sacramento Bee Collection, Sacramento Archives and Museum Collection Center.*

W ho came to the Memorial Auditorium? Who were those who walked between the entry columns and sat in the arena for a boxing match, a concert, or folk dance festival? They may have been the city mayor, a clothing store owner, a cannery worker with her children on her day off from the steaming tomato canning line, the school superintendent and his wife, a foundry worker and his locomotive mechanic buddy from the Southern Pacific shops, or teenagers hanging out together during their summer vacation.

In some very real ways, the Memorial Auditorium and its wide variety of offerings directly reflected the great mixture of people, nationalities, occupations, and talents present in Sacramento during the height of its uses. Legislators from the Capitol and box makers from the canneries, Polish, Greek, Chinese, Slovakian, English, Portuguese, and Armenian immigrants found work in Sacramento's community with its broad base of agriculture, transportation, and state politics. The auditorium became the heart and soul of this diverse Sacramento. The events that drew people through its doors also drew the community together, lending, despite its position as the state capital, and its transient farm population, the strong small-town ambience where most people knew each other, or at least saw each other at the auditorium.

A full house for the opera. *Sacramento Bee*

DECADE TWO: 1937 - 1947

WAR YEARS

I n Washington, D.C. in 1937, a newly re-elected Franklin D. Roosevelt was looking back upon his first term in office with a flush of success. He had instituted several programs during his first four years that were bringing the country out of the Depression and putting thousands of people back to work. In Europe, Adolf Hitler, who for several years had been arousing the German people with his oratory, began viewing his neighbors with the lustful eyes of conquest. Meanwhile, in Northern California the Sacramento Memorial Auditorium was beginning its second decade as the city's premier entertainment venue and community hall.

For the auditorium, the decade had begun with its two-month closure for acoustical remodeling. The following year it was reroofed. The events on the auditorium calendar echoed those of the first decade until December 7, 1941, when war-related activities were added. Conventions, concerts, balls, sporting events, and graduations remained the staples, supplemented during the war years with USO dances, bond drives, and harvest festivals. Governor Culbert Olson held his inaugural in the auditorium in January 1939. The KFBK orchestra, under the direction of Emil Martin, played for the event. Youthful Ruth O'Kane was the vocalist; now Ruth Byrne, she remembers the occasion well.

In January 1940, as the atmosphere was heating up in Europe, Sacramento held its eighth annual sports carnival in the auditorium, drawing capacity crowds. The carnival featured a snow queen contest, a professional vaudeville show, and performances by the

Governor Olson's inauguration, January 1939. *Sacramento Bee.*

A child awaits re-location. *Sacramento Ethnic Survey Collection, Sacramento Archives and Museum Center.*

Sacramento Symphony Ballet, as well as a ski equipment show. Later that month, President Roosevelt's birthday was celebrated with the annual President's Birthday Ball benefiting local victims of infantile paralysis.

The Japanese attack on Pearl Harbor not only brought the United States actively into the conflict but created a national hysteria in the country that resulted in the wholesale evacuation of people of Japanese descent in California and other parts of the country. In Sacramento, notices were posted in early May 1942 instructing "all persons of Japanese ancestry" to evacuate. They were given one week to close their businesses and dispose of their property. Sacramento's 3,800 Japanese-American citizens began registering at the Memorial Auditorium on the morning of May 8. On the thirteenth, I Street between 15th and 16th, and 15th Street between I and J, were blocked to traffic as the first day of the evacuation began. With only their essential personal possessions packed in baggage that they could carry themselves, 825 Japanese-American men, women and children were loaded on buses and taken to the assembly camp at Walerga (near today's intersection of I-80 and Madison Avenue). For three days, buses filled with Japanese-American families and their belongings made trip after trip between the auditorium and Walerga, where the families would stay until transported to permanent relocation centers for the remainder of the war.

But the war years also brought more positive uses. For two years the auditorium served as a dormitory for soldiers. Beds arranged in the basement accommodated approximately 175 servicemen who came to Sacramento every Saturday night. Another frequent war-time event at the auditorium, USO dances, often combined with a war bond or a recruiting drive. Actresses doing double-duty as "pin-up girls" sometimes appeared at the dances to help with the entertainment and recruitment; at other times Sacramento women served as hostesses. Local orchestras provided the music. John and Katerine Graham met at the first USO dance, held in November 1941. For the grand march the men were lined up on one side of the room and the women on the other. When the lines came together, John and Katerine ended up as partners. They have been partners ever since. Another such affair, sponsored by the *Sacramento Bee*, radio station KFBK, and the USO on November 1, 1944 featured a Halloween theme. The auditorium was decorated with cornstalks, scarecrows, and pumpkins, and all service men and women and their spouses or sweethearts were invited. One thousand USO host-

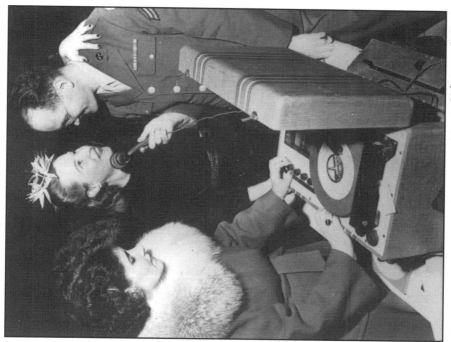

Volunteers helped make voice recordings the servicemen could send home. *McClatchy Collection, Sacramento Archives and Museum Collection Center.*

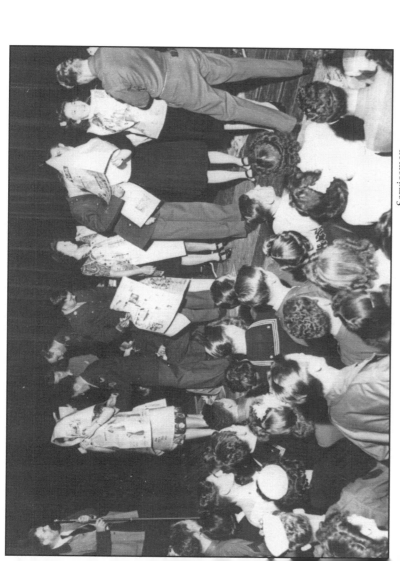

esses also attended. Several hilarious games afforded the participants the chance to win such prizes as war bonds, war stamps, and phone calls home. Another feature of the party was the opportunity to make a five-minute voice recording to mail home.

Fighting men were not the only ones for whom recruitment events were held in the auditorium. In 1944 nearly four thousand people attended an Army

Servicemen attempt to create costumes for female contestants, using newspaper as the only material. The best costume created within the time limit won. *McClatchy Collection, Sacramento Archives and Museum Collection Center.*

Thousands of people attended the Victory Harvest Festivals. *Sacramento Bee.*

Mr. G.B. Cordano won several ribbons for his entries. His garden, in the vacant lot adjoining his house, was judged the best individual garden over 1000 square feet. *Photo and ribbon courtesy of Al Tognotti.*

Sacramento Victory Garden Harvest Festival

Sponsored by
The Sacramento Bee and KFBK

• THIRD AWARD •

Memorial Auditorium
Aug. 5-6, 1943

show featuring big band music, military films, and rifle drills to recruit harvest and cannery workers. Big war bond drives attracted some "big name" entertainers to the auditorium: Ronald Coleman, Louise Reiner, Georgie Jessel, Red Skelton, Kathryn Grayson, and Robert Preston all participated. Dancing to the KFBK orchestra followed the acts by the stars.

Actress Claire Trevor joined war heroes and civic leaders in a "Food for Victory" rally held in the auditorium in July 1943. The purpose of the rally was to recruit volunteers for the crop harvest, as there was a shortage of farm labor. The next month, a Victory Garden Harvest Festival at the auditorium encouraged and brought together the harvests of Victory gardeners and the backyard farmers program throughout the valley. Sponsored by the *Bee* and KFBK, it was a huge event with approximately thirteen thousand county residents attending. County Supervisor Henry Senf commented that the "exhibit [was] not only revealing of the productivity of the county's soil but also is inspirational in that it shows the spirit of cooperation of the residents in this area." Again, Emil Martin's KFBK orchestra with vocalists Ruth O'Kane and Paul Putnam entertained. Judges handed out war bonds, war stamps, plaques, and ribbons as prizes.

A second, much larger, harvest festival was held in 1944. In addition to the vast amounts of produce on

Frank Sinatra on stage in the Memorial Auditorium. *Andy Flink.*

display, the continuous entertainment, and the films in the Little Theater, that year's festival included a broadcast from the auditorium of "America's Town Meeting of the Air." Nearly two thousand attended the broadcast. The Right Reverend Robert Armstrong, bishop of the Sacramento Catholic Diocese, was one of the winners that year. He was awarded ribbons for the crooked-neck and hubbard squash he grew in his victory garden at 2030 Capitol Avenue.

The week after the harvest festival, the army put on a huge show at the auditorium to again recruit harvest and cannery workers. Participants in the show rolled into town in a convoy of approximately twenty vehicles of every sort, ranging from a scout car to three-quarter ton weapon carriers filled with armament. The show included war department films, bands, rifle drills, first aid demonstrations simulating battlefield conditions, and talks by war heroes.

Nor did the war interrupt the regular entertainment events at the auditorium. Boxing and wrestling continued to draw enthusiastic fans. In 1942, a near-record boxing crowd of 4,619 watched what was dubbed the "great grudge go" for the Sacramento middleweight title. The evening of fights included at least one unscheduled bout. Between the preliminaries and the main bout two fans tangled for about five minutes in the gallery. When one of them got the upper hand, and a free-for-all was threatened, "a

squad of policemen attacked and packed the impromptu battler out feet first."[1] When an exciting match between Lloyd Marshall and Newsboy Millich ended in a seventh-round technical knockout for Marshall, the referee turned out to be the most injured man in the ring and was taken to the hospital with two cracked ribs from a wild punch. In 1946, the famous Joe Louis fought an exhibition match in the building.

Although many stars toured the military camps and entertained the troops both at home and abroad, concerts, circuses, and the like also maintained nearly normal schedules. In 1943, a record crowd of eight thousand turned out to see Harry James. Marilyn Hornbeck remembers going to "big band" concerts at the auditorium in the 1940s. Marilyn was an avid baseball fan and spent her summer days at Cardinal (later Edmonds) Field. She became friends with Cecelia and Leroy "Shorty" Jordan who both worked at the park. Shorty operated the scoreboard there, but he also worked as a security person at the auditorium. He used to let fourteen-year-old Marilyn sneak into the concerts through the side door, then escort her home afterwards. In addition to Harry James, Marilyn remembers seeing the bands of Vaughn Monroe, Tommy Dorsey, Jimmy Dorsey, Gene Krupa, and Chico Marx, and singers Frank Sinatra and Mel Tormé. In fact, she recalls that the first time she saw Tormé he was a drummer, not a singer.

The 1943-44 Sacramento Music Series featured the San Francisco Opera Company's productions of Puccini's *Girl of the Golden West* and *La Boheme* with Ezio Pinza, the Baccaloni Opera Company's *Don Pasquale*, the Ballet Theater, and *Porgy and Bess*, in addition to several performing artists. In April 1943, Metropolitan Opera star Risë Stevens, whose husband was stationed at Camp Kohler (previously Walerga), performed operatic selections in a benefit concert with the Camp Kohler Glee Club. Other shows in those years included Lieutenant Rudy Vallee conducting the Coast Guard band, Frank Fay's vaudeville revue "Laugh Time," and Ed Wynn's troupe of comedians, dancers, and singers in a musical revue.

The Shrine circus also maintained its schedule during the war years. Besides its regular acts, in 1943 the circus featured baby elephant twins and a trapeze artist who spent the Sacramento en-

gagement trying in vain to perform a triple somersault, previously accomplished by only one other person. As usual, several thousand orphans and underprivileged children attended as guests of the Shriners.

In 1944, with the casualties from the war mounting, Sacramento again turned its attention to honoring its war dead. American Legion Post 61 proposed that the names of those lost in World War II be installed in the auditorium along with those from the previous wars. In addition, the City Council gave brief consideration to enlarging the auditorium after the war to provide meeting halls and facilities for the veterans' organizations; nothing came of the latter discussions, however.

As the war came to a close, the auditorium's schedule continued to be filled with major entertainment events. In 1945, Mabel Hazelton and Carolyn Ware, the founders and directors of the Music Series, brought the musicals *Desert Song* and *Blossom Time* to Sacramento. Also that year the series featured the famous José Iturbi and his sister, Amparo, in a two-piano recital. So popular was the concert that seats were set up in the orchestra pit and on the stage behind the performers to accommodate the overflow crowd. The following year, Iturbi also set an attendance record for the building. Marian Anderson, Paul Robeson, the Philadelphia Symphony under Eugene

Courtesy of Andy Flink.

A school music festival with choirs on the stage and orchestras in a circle in the center of the floor. *Andy Flink.*

Ormandy, Les Brown, Count Basie, and the Glenn Miller Orchestra—by this time without Glenn Miller—were some of the other major attractions in 1946. Also overflowing the building's capacity in both 1945 and 1946 was the annual Festival of Music program featuring nearly two thousand of the city's junior high, high school, and college music students. The festivals were major events for the city's young musicians. They were broadcast on national radio, and KFBK made recordings that proud parents could purchase.

Sacramento Junior College also held an annual event at the auditorium that was one of the major social events each season throughout the decade. The Junior College Art Ball had originated the year the auditorium was under construction. Organized by the Sacramento Junior College Art League, the ball was held in the auditorium in the 1930s and 1940s. Selection of a queen and her court, dancing, and pageantry of Ziegfeldian proportions, with elaborate costumes and original choreography, culminated a year of planning by student and faculty committees.

Auditorium manager Dewey Baker reported substantially increased revenues at the end of the 1946-1947 fiscal year. Indeed, they exceeded all previous years by a considerable sum. The increase came largely from higher rental rates, but exceeded Baker's esti-

mate. During that fiscal year, there had been thirty-one commercial dances, thirty boxing matches, forty-one wrestling matches, sixteen basketball games, twenty-three operas and concerts, and twenty other entertainment events, including the circus and an ice show, in the auditorium. The major events which played to large houses had contributed most of the excess.

Junior College Arts Ball, November, 1942. Compliments of Violet Phelps.

Decade Three: 1947 - 1957

Years of Promise

The war was over, the boys were home; ration cards and victory gardens would soon be nothing but memories. Returning soldiers who had resumed life and begun families needed homes. Hence, the 1950s were a time of suburban home building in Sacramento with such subdivisions as Arden Park, east of the city, and Parkway Estates in the south area. Town and Country at Fulton and Marconi, one of the first suburban shopping malls in the United States, had just been completed. The decade was off to a great start for Sacramento. It was also off to a great start for the Memorial Auditorium, which began the decade with its highest gross ever. For many years, the revenue from the building's rentals and concession receipts had not been sufficient to pay the operating expenses. The 1946 increase in rent had made a difference; the building was now operating in the black.

In 1949 auditorium superintendent Dewey Baker died, and his post was taken over by Elmer Congdon, who had been assistant superintendent of the City Recreation Department. At the same time, the auditorium's management was moved to the Recreation Department. Congdon would remain as superintendent until he retired in 1956.

Another shot was taken at the auditorium's acoustics in 1952. The Saturday Club, sponsors of one of

the concert series that used the building, urged the city to hire a consultant to find a way to improve the acoustics for concerts. An acoustical shell was seen as the answer, and in 1953 the shell was erected. To aid the situation, in 1955 the city purchased a new sound system for the building. The new equipment was given its first test at the vaudeville show during Southern Pacific Company's employee party; everybody approved.

When City Manager Bartley Cavanaugh suggested that beer be sold at public events in the building, the issue caused a major ruckus at a January 1957 City Council meeting. Overwhelming opposition made Cavanaugh withdraw the proposal, but the protesters would have their say. One man vehemently against the idea, took Cavanaugh to task for the idea, impugning his character in the process. In a heated exchange, Cavanaugh defended himself, and several councilmen spoke on his behalf. When the protester attempted to leave the podium, Mayor Clarence Azevedo shouted, "Come back here. We're not through with you yet." While the man stood subdued, the mayor and three more councilmen continued with the defense of Cavanaugh.

Musicals, such as *South Pacific*, *Show Boat*, *Carousel*, *Oklahoma*, and *Kiss Me Kate* came to the auditorium during these years, as did great names in modern

CHAPTER 9

Musical Memories

Buddy Harpham played saxophone and clarinet for George Breece's KFBK orchestra in the late 1930s and early 1940s, until he was called up during the war. The orchestra folded in the later years of the war for lack of musicians. By the time the war ended, the radio station had made other arrangements for its music and stopped using a live orchestra. Buddy, however, continued his musical career, forming his own orchestra and often playing at the Memorial Auditorium. He played dances, such as the Trianon Ball, parties, proms, concerts, and graduations there. He also played for vaudeville shows, ice shows, western shows, and the circus. The circus brought their own conductor, drummer, organist, and sometimes first trumpeter, but hired local musicians for the rest of the orchestra. Beginning in the 1950s, the circus hired members of the Shrine band, as much as possible. One of the more unusual events Buddy remembers playing for was the Lipizzaner Stallion Show at the auditorium.

Practical Jokers

The unwary often found themselves the butt of jokes played by the auditorium staff. John Cox, for many years the building's head stagehand, told of a prank frequently played on newcomers. A chair or bench conveniently located backstage was wired from beneath to give an electrical shock to anyone taking a seat. An unsuspecting guest, invited to sit down for a moment, got quite a surprise and found him or herself the object of great amusement.

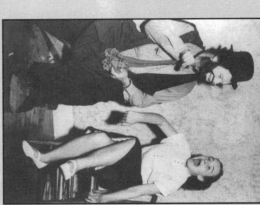

Courtesy of John Cox.

John's father, Francis Cox, was head stagehand for many years before his son took over. At much the same time (1949, 1956), Elmer Congdon was the building manager. One of the custodians on the staff during those years was a man who, unfortunately for him, was quite easily startled. According to Congdon's son, Ralph, his father and the elder Cox, obviously not men to pass up an opportunity for a good laugh, would sneak up behind the unwary fellow and set off a firecracker. The prank undoubtedly did nothing to assuage the poor man's jumpiness.

Even dignitaries did not escape the mischief. Congdon, although a non-drinker himself, was asked to keep liquor on hand for privileged visitors. He purchased bottles of inexpensive brands and kept them in a cabinet. One official, who liked only the best, brought his own bottle of Wild Turkey and asked the manager to save it exclusively for him and his guests. After several visits, when the bottle began to run low, Congdon refilled it with whatever was in the cabinet. The next time the fellow stopped by, Congdon poured him a glass of "Brand X" from the Wild Turkey bottle; the official never knew the difference.

Sacramento Bee.

music. The appearances in the auditorium of the King Cole Trio, the Ink Spots, Louis Armstrong, and Mel Tormé were indicative of the rising popularity of vocal jazz nationwide. Also in these years, Duke Ellington, Dizzy Gillespie, Gene Krupa, Woody Herman, Lionel Hampton, and Stan Kenton appeared, bringing instrumental jazz to Sacramento audiences. Tommy Dorsey, Benny Goodman, and Paul Whiteman and his orchestra, playing an all-Gershwin program, continued the tradition of big band music. Artur Rubenstein, Eugene Ormandy and the Philadelphia Symphony, the Vienna Boys Chorus, and the Sacramento Philharmonic were among the classical concerts. Musical events in a lighter vein were Spike Jones Shows and the Grand Ole Opry.

Wrestling fans watched Gorgeous George at the auditorium in 1951. Boxing remained a regular sporting event in the form of the Tuesday night fights, but the Olympic Trials, held in the auditorium in June 1948, no doubt provided one of the decade's highlights. The Harlem Globetrotters and Donkey Basketball provided basketball events for the whole family. Car shows had also become a annual offering on the auditorium's schedule, and for auto enthusiasts the highlight was probably the showing of the Tucker auto, of which only fifty-one were ever produced.

Community events also remained a major item on the auditorium's schedule. In 1948 the students in the city schools participated in a special pageant celebrating California's 100th birthday. Every year at holiday time, both the *Sacramento Bee* and the Department of Parks and Recreation put on Christmas shows. The Bee show was *for* the youngsters, while the recreation department's show *featured* young people from their tap, ballet, modern, and acrobatic dancing classes. Events like these gave the city's youth the opportunity to perform in this huge hall, where many of them had already seen major productions staged.

While this was the decade of recovery and excitement that followed the end of World War II, it was also the decade of the Korean War and the explosion of the first hydrogen bomb at Eniwetok Atoll in 1951. It was at this time, too, that Memorial Hall, to the left of the lobby, was turned into an air defense center, with tables of maps and charts filling the room. Another notable event that took place during this ten-year period was the inauguration of Goodwin Knight when he succeeded Earl Warren as governor of California, after Warren was appointed to the Supreme Court in 1953.

96

THE SACRAMENTO PHILHARMONIC ASSOCIATION

1947-1948

PRESENTS THE

SYMPHONY SERIES OF THE

Sacramento
Philharmonic Orchestra

GEORGE BARR, CONDUCTOR

PAULENA CARTER, PIANO SOLOIST
FEBRUARY 19, 1948
MEMORIAL AUDITORIUM, SACRAMENTO
8:30 P.

The Sacramento Philharmonic played regularly in the auditorium. Program and photo, Bonnie Snyder Collection.

Rehearsal of a candy cane dance for performance in the annual Christmas show at the Memorial Auditorium, by students of the recreation department's dance classes. Sacramento Bee.

The Romance of Ushering

Ushering at the auditorium runs in Hilda Kerfoot's family. Her father, Hubert Schumacher, had been an usher there, before Hilda followed in his footsteps in the late 1940s. Cal Kerfoot got involved in ushering through his church. Cal worked the balconies, while Hilda's area was the dress circle. Cal spotted Hilda, got introduced, and invited her to his youth group meetings. Since ushers had to remain on duty only until all were seated or the first act had ended, Hilda would save Cal a seat in the dress circle. The pair married sometime later, but kept ushering.

Ushers did not get paid in those days, but they got to see the shows. They also dressed up for their job. Most of the time the men wore sport jackets and the women, dresses, but for the opera, tuxedos and formal gowns were required. As the newlyweds did not have much money, it was a great way for them to enjoy some of the marvelous entertainers and shows that visited Sacramento.

Hilda and Cal had two sons who eventually also ushered at the auditorium. The young men helped out primarily at sporting events, such as Globetrotter exhibitions and table tennis matches. Ushering must have been in their blood.

In 1956, when Elmer Congdon retired, the convention bureau took over the operation of the auditorium. As the decade turned, the *Bee* noted the auditorium's anniversary with an article chronicling its history and its thirty years as the city's premier entertainment and convention venue.

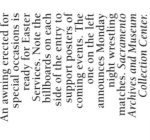

An awning erected for special occasions is ready for Easter Services. Note the billboards on each side of the entry to support posters of coming events. The one on the left announces Monday night wrestling matches. *Sacramento Archives and Museum Collection Center.*

CAMELLIA FESTIVAL

Camellias have been an important flower in Sacramento since shortly after the Gold Rush. Mayor A. E. Goddard attempted to dub Sacramento the "Camellia City" in 1910 when he had postcards of the city printed up depicting it as such. The camellia would have to wait until 1941, however, before the city council formally adopted it as Sacramento's official flower and "Camellia City" became the city's rightful nickname. But long before the name, there was the annual camellia show. The Sacramento Garden Club, and after 1943, the Sacramento Camellia Society, have been staging the shows every year since 1924, with the exception of 1933 when a heavy freeze destroyed the buds.

Thinking that Sacramento needed a major event around which the community could rally, Edmond A. Combatalade conceived the idea of a festival built around the camellia. He soon interested some other people in the idea and formed the Sacramento Camellia Festival Association. In 1955, the association held the first Camellia Festival. Combatalade, who remained active in the festival for nearly twenty years, became known as "Camellia Ed" and "Mr. Camellia" for his efforts.

The main events in the early years of the festival were the Camellia Show, the queen contest, the ball, the parade, the luncheon and fashion show, and the Folk Dance Pageant. The queen and her court of princesses were chosen each year from entrants from the community colleges and from Sacramento State College (now California State University, Sacramento). Prominent Sacramento business and professional men served as escorts for the queen and her princesses, escorting them to functions and events associated with the festival. In 1964, the escorts donned the gold jackets with which they would forever after be associated. The jackets gained for the escorts the name "Golden Boys," which later, gratefully, gave way to the moniker "Gold Coaters."

The Folk Dance Pageant introduced an international theme to the festival which became a hallmark of the event. Each year one of the countries represented in the Sacramento Folk Dance Council was selected to be the honored country. The parade and often the theme of the festival itself, were centered around the honored country, and the folk dancers representing the country were invited to appear at other events. An International Friendship Luncheon helped celebrate the international aspect of the festival.

The Camellia Show and the Folk Dance Festival were always held in the Memorial Auditorium. The ball was held there for many years, and other events associated with the festival also used the auditorium for their functions over the years. The folk dancers enjoyed dancing on the auditorium floor. Dorothy Carr, a longtime member of the Scottish folk dancers group, remembers that she could feel it move when all the dancers were performing together. The 1986 Folk Dance Festival was the very last event held at the auditorium before it closed down. The city informed the folk dance council that the building was closing and they would not be able to hold the festival there. The folk dance council talked the city into holding off the closure until after the festival since they would not be able to find another place on short notice. So while the great flood of 1986 was in progress, the festival staged the auditorium's last hurrah before its ten-year sleep.

Folk Dance Festival performance on main floor of auditorium. *Sacramento Bee Collection, Sacramento Archives and Museum Collection Center.*

After the auditorium closed in 1986, the Camellia *Show* moved to the Sacramento Community Center and the Folk Dance *Festival* to various other venues, and both still take place every year. However, although the Camellia *Festival* continued for several more years, the auditorium's closure really sang its swan song.

Camellia Show set up on the main floor of the auditorium in 1968. *Sacramento Bee Collection (Leo Neibaur), Sacramento Archives and Museum Collectin Center.*

Van Cliburn signing autographs for young fans. *Andy Flink.*

Decade Four: 1957 - 1967

Years of Change

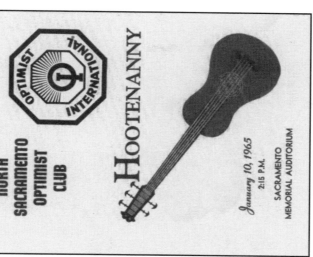

Peter, Paul, and Mary performing at the Memorial Auditorium in 1970 (above left). *Dennis Warren.* Program from Soroptimist Hootenanny (above). *Sacramento Archives and Collection Center.*

By the late 1950s the Cold War dominated international relations. Americans, fearful that the hydrogen bomb could wipe out the country, built bomb shelters in their communities and held air raid drills in their schools. In January 1957, Dwight Eisenhower was sworn in for his second term as President, and in 1958, Goodwin Knight began his first full term as governor of California.

The Civil Rights Movement, the election of President John F. Kennedy in 1960, his assassination in 1963, and the escalation of fighting in Vietnam brought the youth of this country into social and political awareness and action. Their social consciousness was reflected in the so-called "folk music revival," which began in the 1950s with political balladeers such as Pete Seeger and Woody Guthrie, and groups such as The Weavers. Joan Baez and Bob Dylan continued the tradition, becoming cult figures with their compelling protest music. In the late 1950s, the movement was popularized by the Kingston Trio's recording of "Tom Dooley," and the establishment of folk festivals and hootenannies across the country.

In 1965, the North Sacramento Optimist Club staged a hootenanny in the auditorium for local folk sing-

ing groups. It was by far the largest hall in which many of the groups had ever, or would ever, appear. John Snyder, who played banjo with one of the participating groups, the Glendyburke Singers, remembers the thrill of being on the same stage where he had watched the Kingston Trio and Peter, Paul, and Mary perform. In fact, one of the times John saw the Kingston Trio at the auditorium, the warm-up act was a comedy routine by a young, unknown come-

CHAPTER 10

Tickets to the three-day reopening weekend were free from local merchants.

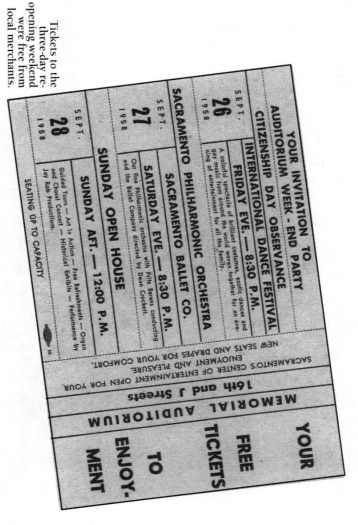

YOUR INVITATION TO
AUDITORIUM WEEK - END PARTY
CITIZENSHIP DAY OBSERVANCE
INTERNATIONAL DANCE FESTIVAL

SEPT. 26 1958
FRIDAY EVE.— 8:30 P.M.
A colorful spectacle of brilliant costume, exotic dances and gay music from around the world woven together for an evening of entertainment for all the family.

SACRAMENTO PHILHARMONIC ORCHESTRA

SEPT. 27 1958
SATURDAY EVE.— 8:30 P.M.
Our fine Philharmonic orchestra with Fritz Berens conducting and the Ballet Company directed by Dean Crockett.

SACRAMENTO BALLET CO.

SEPT. 28 1958
SUNDAY OPEN HOUSE
SUNDAY AFT.— 12:00 P.M.
Guided Tours — Art in Action — Free Refreshments — Organ and Choral Concert — Historical Exhibits — Performance by Jar Rob Productions.

SEATING UP TO CAPACITY

12

YOUR FREE TICKETS TO ENJOY-MENT

MEMORIAL AUDITORIUM

16th and J Streets

SACRAMENTO'S CENTER OF ENTERTAINMENT OPEN FOR YOUR ENJOYMENT AND PLEASURE.
NEW SEATS AND DRAPES FOR YOUR COMFORT.

they felt would go well with the gold and green of the existing decoration. The stage curtains and those along the orchestra rail would be turquoise; the 2,544 new seats, rust. The committee also recommended that the rest of the interior decor be changed over time to harmonize with the new colors. The remodeling would also include an updating of the heating system, a new public address system, renovated restrooms, repainting on the main floor, and the addition of a ramp for those with disabilities. The building was closed for the months of July, August, and part of September 1958, while the alterations were made.

The huge reopening celebration was a three-day event, dubbed the Auditorium Week-end Party. Timed to correspond with Citizenship Day, the event opened on Friday, September 26 with an International Dance Festival sponsored by the Northern California Conference on Citizenship. On Saturday there were performances by the Sacramento Philharmonic Orchestra and the Sacramento Ballet. Sunday was open house day with guided tours of the building including a demonstration of the raising and lowering of the floor, organ and choral concerts, and a play by JayRob Productions in the Little Theater Arts and historical exhibitions were on view in the meeting rooms throughout the weekend. Admission to the whole weekend was free, but tickets available from downtown merchants were required. It was a

dian named Bill Cosby. The Limeliters were another popular folk-singing trio to appear at the auditorium. Their 1962 show, scheduled for December 15, had to be postponed until January 17, 1963, because they were injured in a plane crash on December 12.

For the auditorium at the beginning of the decade, another remodeling was in the offing. In July 1957, Mayor Clarence Azevedo appointed a committee to recommend color schemes for new seats and curtains. They chose the trendy shades of the day, which

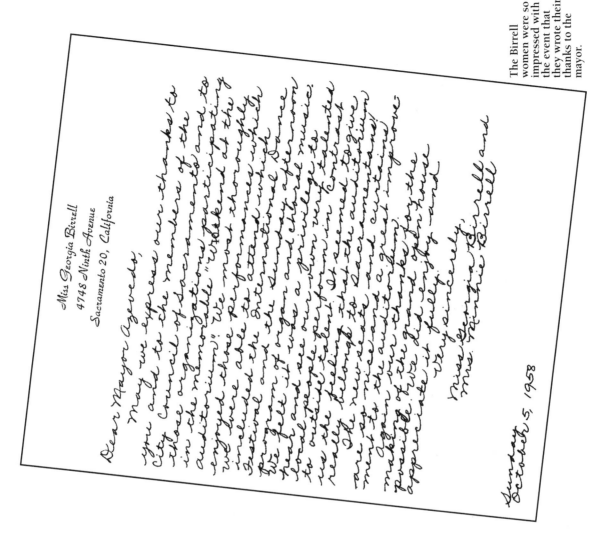

The Birrell women were so impressed with the event that they wrote their thanks to the mayor.

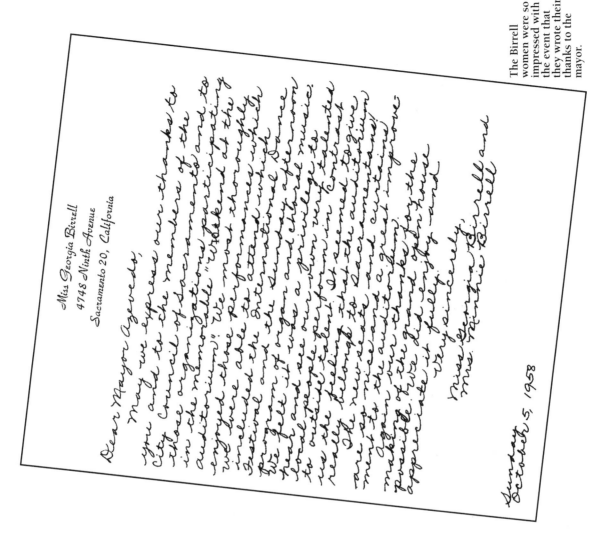

major success with approximately 8,500 Sacramentans attending over the three-day period. One attendee wrote to thank those responsible. She said seeing local talent perform there made her feel that the auditorium really belonged to Sacramentans. The building's original planners would have been pleased.

It may have been the wrong time to refurbish and get new seats. Although symphony and opera aficionados continued to frequent their favorite events, popular music had changed: Jazz and folk singers replaced the orchestra-backed vocalists. The ballroom dances common to the 1930s and 1940s had faded out of popularity after the war. Now, a new breed of dance music supplanted the big bands, and with it came a new breed of young dancers. Rock'n'roll, ushered in with the success of such hits as "Shake, Rattle and Roll" (1954), and "Rock Around the Clock" (1955), by Bill Haley and the Comets, not only changed music but changed entirely the style of dancing from that of the big band era. Out went the fox trot, in came the twist.

Whether it was the music, or the dancing, or just something about the times, dances also seemed to be much rowdier affairs. In Sacramento at the end of 1959, the aftermath of the dances was even worse. After a dance at the auditorium in October, two men driving by in their cars were beaten up by three young attackers. The police chief, who had already increased the number of officers patrolling the area after dances, ordered suspicious cars filled with youths stopped for questioning, and street gatherings dispersed. The *Sacramento Union* commented, "...if rock'n'roll has such a violent effect upon its disciples, it is fortunate that some of us were tripping the light fantastic, not under such stimulation, but in the era of the soothing Strauss waltz...."[1] Despite the police department's additional efforts, riots broke out after the New Year's Eve dance, injuring five policemen. Another editorial in the *Union* called the dances at the auditorium a municipal disgrace. Contrasting the event with the "Chesterfieldian social code associated with the ballroom in days more staid," the editor suggested that, "A visitor from Mars, chancing to drop in at Memorial Auditorium on New Year's Eve after the ball was over, would have been mystified by the conduct at this public social event. For that matter, so would an interloper from a previous generation of earthmen."[2] Although Bert Geisreiter, the building manager, worried that the building's reputation was being damaged—and it well may have been—it also seems likely that the auditorium itself suffered; over three hundred empty liquor bottles were cleaned out of the building the next day. The City Council voted unanimously to suspend rock'n'roll dances for six months.

It was not only the dances that got out of hand; so did concerts. In the early 1960s, three musical brothers named Wilson, a cousin and a friend, formed the extremely popular group known as the Beach Boys. The group brought surfing music to the attention of the country with their "Surfer Girl" and "Surfin' USA." A college student named Frederick Vail got the Beach Boys to come to Sacramento and then promoted several more of their concerts here and elsewhere. Wally Clark, now owner of a sound equipment business in Sacramento, was a friend of Vail's who remembers getting into one of the concerts free because his father's company printed the posters. With his earnings, Vail bought himself a midnight blue, 1963 split-window Corvette Stingray coupe, just like the one Dennis Wilson had.

In 1963, at Vail's suggestions, the Beach Boys recorded their first live album, "Beach Boys Concert," in the building. About two hours before the show thousands of fans were already lined up around the block. While audience reaction was part of a live concert that was often boosted mechanically, for this album the audience response was so overwhelming that Capitol Record Company's recording engineers had to *subdue* audience sounds and enhance the vocal and instrumental portions.

The Beach Boys loved playing Sacramento because of the great enthusiasm of the fans. It was so great, in fact, that for one concert, the riot squad had to be called. While the entertainers surely appreciated their fans' enthusiasm, the auditorium management did not. The maintenance staff reported that the crowds

Fred and The Boys

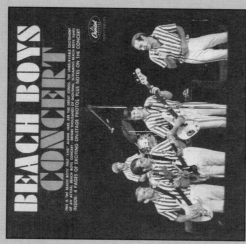

The Beach Boys cut their first live album at their concert in the Memorial Auditorium in 1963. The back of the cover featured the crowd waiting outside.

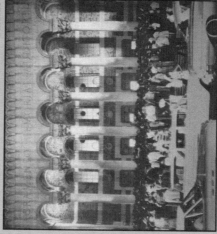

When Fred Vail ran for Commissioner of Entertainment at El Camino in his senior year, he promised to bring big name entertainment to the school assemblies. He won the election and fulfilled his promise. Fred then moved on to graduation parties, booking names such as Jerry Wallace and Bobby Freeman (Do Ya Wanna Dance?) As a freshman at Sacramento State he booked the Four Freshmen among others.

When the El Camino Class of '63 approached Vail for entertainment at their graduation party, Fred suggested that they take the funds they had raised so far and parlay them into enough for a good party by putting on a concert. Fred handled all the details and booked the Beach Boys for May 24. "The Boys" had never toured but had put out a couple of minor albums and had a following in several cities, including Sacramento.

Fred picked the group up at the airport in his old Chevy wagon, loading all their equipment in the back. "The Boys" were surprised to learn they were not only the headliners but the only act on the program. They played their entire repertoire in the first set, so after the intermission they had to repeat some numbers and play some things they were just working on. The concert, which cost $1.75 to attend, was a huge success. "The Boys" themselves were amazed at the crowd and ended up hiring Fred to book more concerts for them. He brought them to Sacramento again in September and December of 1963 and May of the following year. Their first live album, also Fred's suggestion, was recorded at the December and May concerts. Vail's voice can be heard on the album as an announcer.

The concert not only launched "The Boys'" touring career, but also ushered in the era of rock'n'roll concerts at the auditorium. Fred's association with the Beach Boys lasted for many years. He was their manager from 1969-1971. Vail also promoted other artists, booking about a dozen concerts into the auditorium between 1963 and 1966, including Jan and Dean who also recorded part of their live album there in 1964.

KROY RADIO PRESENTS

THE BEACH BOYS

Plus

PAUL REVERE *and* THE RAIDERS

AND

NORTHERN CALIFORNIA'S MOST TALKED ABOUT VOCAL INSTRUMENTAL GROUP

The Marauders

Sat., Feb. 27

7:00 & 9:30 P.M.

SACRAMENTO MEMORIAL AUDITORIUM

Tickets Available at:

Civic Theater Box Office 15th & H Street — 441-3163 and its Agencies Jack's House of Music Knight & Knabe — Rancho Cordova: Aerojet Recreation Center; Freeborn Hall — U.C. Davis.

Courtesy of Wally Clark.

A Picture of Home

In the mid-1960s, when Sacramento-native Dennis Warren was twenty-one, he found himself working in the Boston area and missing Sacramento. One day he happened into a record store in Harvard Square and noticed the newly-released *Beach Boys' Concert* album. Although not really a Beach Boys fan, Dennis picked the album up and looked at it. When he turned it over, he saw a full page photo of the Memorial Auditorium: a picture of "home." To that homesick youth, that beautiful building took on an extra special meaning, reminding him of the hometown he had left behind and missed so much.

Mick Jagger at the auditorium with The Rolling Stones in 1966. *Nicoletta Anselmo.*

Nonetheless, from this time on, the building was a major venue for rock music concerts. The Righteous Brothers, the Dave Clark Five, Herman's Hermits, and the Who were among other groups who appeared there in the 1960s. Sonny and Cher arrived for their concert on a motorcycle so covered with mud that Nate Gourvitch, who for over twenty years supervised the stagehands for many of the events there, nearly threw them out.

According to Fred Vail, the Rolling Stones were on the Ed Sullivan Show on a Sunday in about 1964, then flew to Sacramento and performed their first live concert in the United States in the auditorium. The promoters charged considerably more for the concert than local fans were used to paying, with the result that the crowd inside was smaller than the crowd outside throwing rocks at the building in protest. In December 1965, the Stones included Sacramento in their second tour of the United States, giving two concerts: the second, a very short one that were "very dirty and wild." The seats were soiled from having been stood on, cushions were cut and legs broken off in the orchestra and first balcony, and backs pulled loose from the wooden second-balcony seats.

no one who attended will ever forget. About four songs into the concert, Keith Richards stepped up to the microphone, which happened to be improperly grounded. As he reached the mike, it arced with his guitar and the jolt of electricity sent him staggering to the stage floor. Some who were in the audience recall seeing a blue flash, or sparks, and wondered if Richards was dead. Jeff Hughson, who in 1968 would help found KZAP radio, then work for many years as a concert promoter, heard a loud crack that sounded to him like a pistol shot. Fearing the worst, he turned to his friend and said, "Oh no, somebody just shot Keith Richards. Now no band will ever play Sacramento again." Mick Martin, one-time film reviewer for the *Sacramento Union*, now leader of "Mick Martin's Blues Rockers" and host of Mick Martin's Blues Party on KXJZ, was another of those in attendance. He and his friends ran outside to the stage door and watched Richards being carried out on a stretcher, looking rather blue. The concert, of course, ended then and there, and nobody got rainchecks or refunds—another reason to remember the event!

While folk musicians and rock'n'roll groups were well represented in these years, many other groups and individuals also graced the auditorium stage. Barbra Streisand included Sacramento on her first concert tour in the early 1960s. She had just finished appearing in "I Can Get It For You Wholesale" on Broadway but was not very well-known here and sang

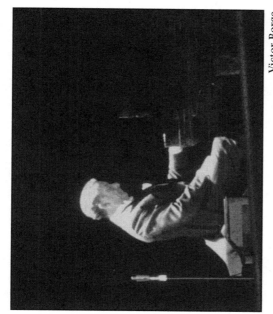

Victor Borge performing at the auditorium in 1965. *Andy Flink.*

to an unfortunately small audience in the big hall. The enduring entertainers were also still appearing, as were the symphony, opera, ballet, musical comedies, and the like. Marian Anderson, who appeared in the auditorium in the 1930s, also appeared in the 1960s. Likewise, Jose Iturbi appeared in the 1940s as well as the 1960s.

Many well-known entertainers took part in the Memorial Day Telethons broadcast from the auditorium. The banks of telephones were located behind the acts on stage. Television stars such as Dan Blocker and Michael Landon, from the extremely popular show *Bonanza*, appeared in the telethons in the 1960s.

Conventions were always a mainstay of the auditorium's schedule. The auditorium had been built, in large part, to capture the convention business in Northern California. Not surprisingly, the number of conventions Sacramento hosted rose precipitously after the auditorium's completion. The '60s saw greater numbers of both conventions and delegates visit the city than ever before. In 1961, Sacramento hosted 180 conventions with 105,024 delegates; in 1964, there were 204 conventions with 132,500 delegates, although not all of the conventions were held at the auditorium. The conventions were sought and booked by the Convention Bureau. The bureau, originally a department of the Chamber of Commerce, was incorporated as a separate entity

on June 8, 1927—four and one half months after the opening of the auditorium—and the two were, naturally, closely affiliated. But the Convention Bureau truly linked arms with the auditorium on July 1, 1956, when the bureau took over the building's management.

Linked as they were, however, the Convention Bureau's ability to interest organizations in holding their conventions in Sacramento outstripped the city's and the auditorium's ability to accommodate them. Furthermore, the city had an obligation to make sure that community groups had ample opportunity to use the auditorium; no doubt, there were many times when booking dates collided. Thus, in the late 1950s, plans got underway to build a new comunity and convention center. City officials envisioned a multi-building complex that included a theater, an exhibit hall, a meeting hall, and the existing auditorium. The complex was to occupy the four blocks between 15th and 17th Streets and I and L Streets. Four separate buildings would be connected to each other by pedestrian bridges over the streets. It was part of a twenty-year plan that was intended to make Sacramento "The City of Tomorrow."

GROUPIES, SACRAMENTO STYLE

Did you ever hear of the Nurk Twins? That was the first name Paul McCartney and John Lennon used for their group back when they were just a duo. It was also the name taken by two Sacramento teenagers in the late 1960s, Lanette Franklin, who still uses the nickname "Nurk," and her friend Nicoletta Anselmo. They both lived in nearby Carmichael, but spent as much of their time as possible between 1964 and 1968 at the auditorium. For the Nurk Twins, rock music fans in love with the rock stars, the auditorium held a magnetism. They thought of the building as home, even called it "home." When they had tickets for a show there they would go to town early, arrive at the auditorium in the afternoon, and try to pick the lock on the back door to sneak in and hide so they could meet the stars when they came in for the performance. Although they were not often successful at getting in and were always caught by the building management, they kept trying. Once Nicoletta and another friend succeeded in getting in, found their way upstairs, and hid. But after some time passed and they had to use the bathroom, they crept down and were caught.

Meeting the groups was very important to these fans. So was grabbing them, an activity for which front row seats were imperative. If they and their friends couldn't get seats in the front row, Lanette would pretend to be an usher. Carrying a flashlight, she would escort her friends to the front row, then make everyone move over and squish together to fit them in.

When the curtain came down on the Rolling Stones concert in October 1964, they rushed the stage, jumping over the low curtain in front of the orchestra pit. Lanette made it and managed to grab Mick Jagger's foot, but Nicoletta fell and ended

up at the bottom of a pile of people. When she finally got up, the curtain was down, and her wrist was in pain. She and a girl having an asthma attack were escorted out the front to a waiting ambulance. She wore the cast on her fractured wrist as a badge but got grounded and had to miss a Yardbirds concert.

At the Stones' December 3, 1965 concert, Nicoletta, thinking she glimpsed Brian Jones through the closed curtain at intermission, hopped over the curtained rail, ran onto the stage and through the curtain. Brian Jones was nowhere in sight, but Nicoletta was nabbed by building security and thrown out of the concert. She ran around the building banging on every door, crying and begging to be let in but to no avail. She heard the second half of the concert from outside the building that night. Later, during the second show, Keith Richards was nearly electrocuted!

They always rushed out of the building before the end of the last number to get to the stage door before the stars ran out to waiting cars or limousines. After that the girls would hurry around to the hotels where the groups usually stayed and feel the car hoods to see if they were warm, indicating they had recently been driven and thus could be those of the stars they wanted to meet.

After high school, Nicoletta moved away for a while, and Lanette began to attend more concerts at the Sound Factory on Alhambra Boulevard because they had dancing there. But the Memorial Auditorium retained its mystique for the Nurk Twins, and the memories of those years and their exploits in the building are still vivid.

The "Nurk Twins" pose in front of the marquis at 15th and J Streets, in February 1965. *Lanette Franklin.*

The 1960s were years of turmoil, as demonstrated by the literature table for the "Free Speech Movement" in the corridor of the auditorium during the 1966 California Democratic Council convention (left), and the "Women for Peace" march during their 1965 meeting (above). *Dennis Warren.*

Interestingly, although printed material stated that the entrance to the auditorium would be "modified" to relate it to the pedestrian bridge over J Street, none of the accompanying illustrations showed the auditorium from the front or gave any hint as to how the bridge would actually meet and enter it. And for good reason: Clearly such a structure would not only have obscured the auditorium's grand facade but would have seriously damaged it.

The city took the proposal to the voters on February 19, 1965. It was one of several failed attempts to get voter approval for such a project. They would try and fail again in June 1966.

On January 20, 1967, the Convention Bureau hosted a dinner in the Hotel El Rancho in West Sacramento, to jointly celebrate the fortieth birthday of both the bureau and the building which played such an important role in its success.

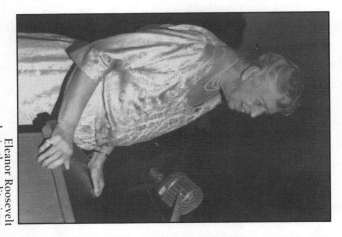

Eleanor Roosevelt spoke in the auditorium in 1960 (above). *Sacramento Bee Collection, Sacramento Archives and Museum Collection Center.* In spite of the rain and a right-wing student group protesting against her support of the U.N., the house was so full that many were turned away (right). *Sacramento Bee.*

Decade Five: 1967 - 1977

The Problem Years

Rock musician Ted Nugent at the Memorial Auditorium in 1977. *Greg Savalin*

For many, especially the youth of the nation, these were not good years. The idealism of the 1960s collapsed into cynicism as the nation's youth discovered they could not really change the world. Anti-war rallies protesting America's involvement in Vietnam, the assassinations of Martin Luther King and Bobby Kennedy, the shooting of students at Kent State University, the deception of the Watergate break-in, and President Nixon's resignation in its aftermath, all came together to deal hope a mighty blow. The cynicism was reflected in the music of the era as folk music faded away and rock became hard rock and acid rock.

The rock audiences in Sacramento were very receptive to the new music, and rock groups enjoyed playing the city. In the late 1960s and the 1970s the auditorium was the major venue for concerts in the area. More than sixty different groups appeared at the auditorium during these years. Among the more popular were Steppenwolf; Lynyrd Skynyrd; Earth, Wind, and Fire; Fleetwood Mac; Jefferson Starship; Van Morrison; Jim Morrison and the Doors; Kraftwerk; Robin Trower; Elvin Bishop; Dave Mason; Electric Light Orchestra; the Tubes; and Tower of Power, who also recorded an album there. Bruce Springsteen played at the auditorium in the mid-

1970s to a small crowd that filled only about one third of the seats. Just two weeks later, however, he appeared on the cover of several major magazines who proclaimed him the next Bob Dylan. Greg Savalin remembers the concert because he jumped on the organ to shake hands with Springsteen. The singer reciprocated by jumping in the orchestra pit to shake the hands of the other fans who had gathered there. Other groups and performers of the generation, but not of the rock movement, such as James Brown, Gordon Lightfoot, Loggins and Messina, and Shadowfax, rounded out the schedule.

Sacramento native Bill Estrada traveled the country working as a stage manager for rock concert promoters LeisureTech, Bill Graham Presents, and Wolf and Rissmiller (then Concert Associates), doing as many as 270 shows in a year, and often coming to Sacramento. The stagehands who worked shows in the auditorium would all climb the metal ladders to the tower and sign their names above the outside door there. While Bill was working for LeisureTech, the Van Morrison concert they produced in the auditorium was their nineteenth sellout in a row there. Bill's job for the companies was to set up the stage and make sure everything was there on time—including the bands. He remembers the night Sly and

CHAPTER II

Johnny Winter
(above) played in
the Memorial
Auditorium in
1973. *Greg Savalin.*

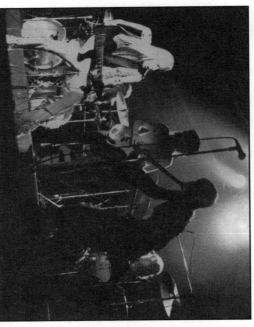

Donovan (below)
was a popular
singer who played
in the auditorium
in September
1968.
Greg Savalin

the Family Stone didn't show up for their performance until an hour and a half after they were scheduled to go on. The crowd got pretty rowdy while they waited. Some impatient fans came up to Bill at the mixing board and threatened him, although there was nothing he could do.

Another no-show was Jim Morrison of the Doors. When the Doors arrived at the Sacramento airport, they discovered Morrison had missed the plane in Los Angeles. At

the auditorium, his group waited for him while the warm-up bands played. One of those bands was The Creators, a local group that included Skip Maggiora, now owner of Skip's Music. Skip remembers that after they and the other warm-up band had finished, they were told to go back on and play some more to appease the crowd, who would not hear the Doors that night. The Creators were delighted, and the audience did not seem to mind either.

With the rock musical *Hair* playing on Broadway, and streakers running naked through public places not an uncommon sight, it was not unusual in those years to see people taking off their clothes at the concerts in the auditorium, dancing around in the aisles, then dressing again before leaving. These were also the years of the groupies waiting outside the stage doors for the stars to exit.

The enthusiasm of the rock fans sometimes went too far. For example, some who could not get into sold-out concerts broke windows attempting to do so. In 1976, controversy arose over the police searching people entering the auditorium for rock concerts. The concert goers were patted down and drugs were confiscated. Bill Estrada knew the policemen who worked the shows very well. He found them to be cordial and polite, although they were often subjected to abuse by the patrons.

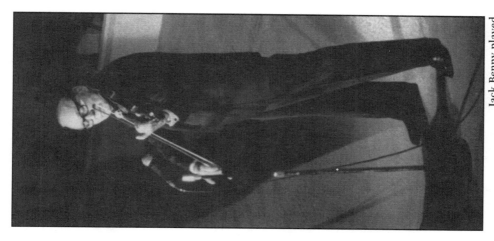

Jack Benny played
his violin at Ronald
Reagan's inaugural
gala in the Memorial
Auditorium in 1971.
Dennis Warren.

The decade brought bad news for the auditorium, too. In 1971, the seating capacity was reduced, because of new fire regulations. The new regulations meant that the only a portion of the 274 temporary seats that were sometimes added at the rear of the house could be utilized. Further, the 300 standing room places and the 116 seats in the orchestra pit could no longer accommodate concert patrons. Seating was restricted to the 4,431 regular seats and 120 temporary seats. Also at this time, the city was gearing up to proceed with the construction of the community center. While planning the construction, the city also considered the auditorium. It was getting old, and it needed repairs and renovation. City officials first considered closing the building and fixing it up while working on the community center. Then because that option would leave the city without a large convention and auditorium space, they considered closing and renovating the auditorium immediately after the completion of the community center. Architect Sookie Lee was hired to draw up some preliminary plans.

In 1974 the Sacramento Community Center, with its convention hall, meeting spaces, and 2,000-seat theater, opened its doors. Long awaited by the performing arts community, the theater immediately became the home of the symphony, which had for many years played many of its concerts in the Sacramento High School auditorium. The ballet and opera were

also delighted to have what they considered to be an acoustically superior venue, with a capacity more suited to its audience. The road companies of the big musical comedies that came to town also switched to the Community Center Theater. Many conventions, too, preferred the shiny new quarters. At that point funds for sprucing up the auditorium were not available, so no work was done on it. Thus the Memorial Auditorium lost some of its business to the new community center. As far as bookings were concerned, the rock concerts were a blessing.

However, there were also other places in town for the rock concerts. The Sound Factory on Alhambra (about where Fort Sutter Post Office is now) was the first venue for some of the major English bands that came to town, such as the original Fleetwood Mac group. Rock concerts had also been booked into Governor's Hall at old fairgrounds. Then in the mid-1960s, Cal Expo opened, and some groups, wanting even bigger halls, went there. One of the things that kept the groups at the auditorium, however, was its own special quality. The rock artists loved the mystique of the auditorium: They appreciated the qualities of the older hall, its beautiful architecture, and how it felt to be there. Their musical style and good equipment overcame the acoustical problems that plagued others. Bill, who not only worked frequently at the auditorium, but had also attended numerous events over the years, feels that going through those

Petition signing in the lobby of the Memorial Auditorium at the Democratic State Convention, 1974. Dennis Warren.

big pillars made you feel like you were really going to see something and added importance to any occasion. Conversely, when Crosby, Stills, and Nash found themselves at Cal Expo, they complained that they had been booked into a cow barn.

Although rock concerts dominated the schedule, in between them were the regulars: the ice shows, circuses, boxing and wrestling matches, roller derbies, basketball games, and annual appearances of the Globetrotters. One of the zanier events was the live, closed circuit telecast of Evel Knievel's motorcycle jump over the Snake River Canyon. Local high school students continued to look forward to attending their proms and graduations at the auditorium.

There were also several important political events held at the auditorium during these years. Vice President Hubert Humphrey

and Secretary of Labor Willard Wirz both attended an AFL/CIO convention there in 1968. In 1971 George McGovern and Alan Cranston were on hand for the California State Democratic Convention. When Ronald Reagan was elected governor, he held his inaugural gala in the auditorium; Frank Sinatra, Jack Benny, and several other of his Hollywood cronies performed. When protesters showed up outside the building, John Wayne went out to say, "Well, listen here...." and had to be restrained by Frank Sinatra from adding action to his words.

At the end of the decade came the truly bad news. The Occupational Safety and Health Administration (OSHA) reported that they were on the verge of condemning the auditorium. Their report found that there were not enough exits, much of the backstage area was obsolete and potentially hazardous, it did not meet seismic codes, and the air conditioning and sprinkler systems were not up to standard. The City Council was told that the building must be renovated or closed. The city applied for $1.8 million of federal job development funds for the project; the rest would have to come from money the city already had. City Hall, in need of similar renovation, was also included in the application for the federal funds. By the end of 1976 the money had not been allocated, but neither was the building closed down.

A pensive George McGovern addressing the California State Democratic Convention at the Mmorial Auditorium, 1971. *Dennis Warren.*

Vice President Hubert Humphrey addressing the AFL/CIO convention held in the Memorial Auditorium in 1968. *Dennis Warren.*

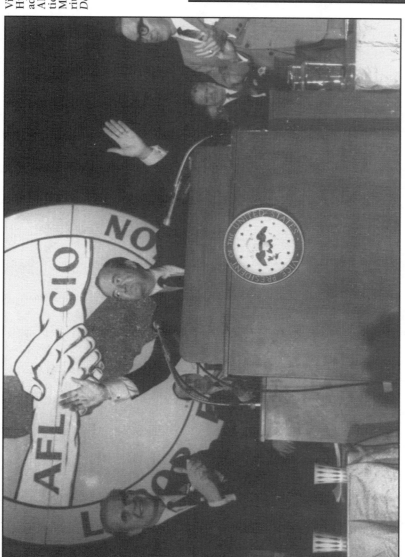

Alan Cranston addressing the Democratic State Convention in 1974. Dennis Warren.

Decade Six: 1977 - 1987

Years of Concern

While concern for the environment began to affect far more Americans than ever before in the aftermath of the nuclear accidents at Three Mile Island and Chernobyl, concern for the future of the auditorium was also on the minds of Sacramento city officials. On the international level, the decade was characterized by hope, as Prince Charles married Diana, and Ronald Reagan won the presidency by a landslide. But it was also tinged with disappointment, as conflicts erupted in Africa and the Middle East, and terrorism increased throughout the world. Conversely, in Sacramento, those connected with the auditorium went from concern and disappointment at having to close it, to hope for its useful future.

Although the building was nominated to the National Register of Historic Places in 1977, the bad news of the previous year did not go away, nor did the list of problems get any shorter. Roof, plumbing, and electrical problems were added to the health and safety violations. Yet, the funding for correcting all the problems was still at issue. Councilman Lloyd Connelly favored using tax-increment money over the federal revenue-sharing dollars, but another year passed with no action. Late in 1978, City Council voted to spend $1.2 million for initial improvements to the audito-

rium during the current fiscal year and an additional $2.4 million for the remaining work over a total of three and one half years. City Engineer Ron Parker told the council that in addition to the necessary repairs previously identified, the renovation would include replacing the 1,500 wooden folding seats with padded ones. Parker explained that the city had gotten numerous complaints from patrons who had gotten splinters or snagged clothing from the fifty-year-old seats. Councilman Roberts agreed that they were "godawful seats."

One year later, the city hired architectural consultants Angello-Vitiello-Niiya-Ryan to study the building and recommend a program for its rehabilitation. In April 1980, the consultants told the city that the repairs would cost $6 million and suggested that they be completed over a period of sixteen months. Assistant City Manager William Edgar called the figures "mind-boggling." He told the City Council that there was $600,000 available to start the work that the city planned as a $5 million project phased over five to ten years. The consultants offered the alternative of phasing the work over twenty-seven months, but warned that it would force the costs up by about $2 million. The report also said that if *everything* was brought up to code in the building, the

Frank Zappa made a hit at the Memorial Auditorium in September 1981. *Dennis Warren.*

Shaffer, reported back to the city, saying, "...we can-not overemphasize the extreme hazard of this heavy ceiling to the public in the event of a major seismic disturbance."[1] Again, the auditorium's renovation was not begun.

Two years later, with the price tag for renovation even higher and the central library in need of expansion, Councilman Terry Kastanis suggested that the audi-torium be converted into the library; His plan would save the city the now $12.7 million in renovation costs—money that could be used to help build a 15,000-25,000-seat sports arena at Cal Expo. City Librarian Robert Richard rejected the idea, however. In January 1986, another idea came up for using the auditorium. The Sacramento Metropolitan Arts Com-mission, holding meetings to get public comment on the arts in Sacramento, heard a suggestion that the building be turned into several small theaters and rehearsal rooms for the performing arts.

Although it had been called a "white elephant" and a drain on the city's resources, the auditorium, un-safe as it was, remained open and in service for three more years. In the intervening time, the fire marshal inspected the building, noting additional safety vio-lations, and a temporary Arco Arena, constructed in North Natomas, satisfied the city's desire for a large sports arena. Also during this time, some Sacramentans, concerned by what they were hear-ing of the building's deficiencies, remembered the

work would "destroy most of the [its] historical fabric and its income-produc-ing capabilities—due to the loss of at least twenty-five percent of its existing seating capacity...." They requested that alternative measures be used that would preserve the architectural integrity of the building while ensuring a "reasonable degree of life safety." The firm said that the ceiling, which had been men-tioned as a major seismic concern, should be removed and replaced with a fiberglass replica. A few months later, the local structural engineering firm of Marr-

Fred Neil of Fred Neil and the Rolling Coconut Band performing at the Save the Whales Concert in the Memorial Auditorium. *Dennis Warren.*

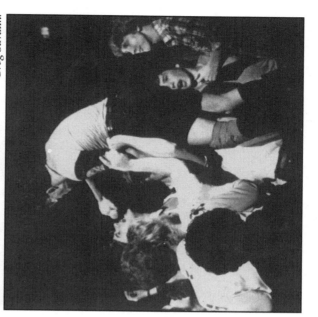

Devo's lead singer with fans at the Memorial Auditorium in early 1980s. *Greg Savalin.*

1973 demolition of the Alhambra Theater to make way for a Safeway market and worried that the auditorium would meet a similar fate. Demolishing the building, however, had not been seriously considered by the city.

While all of this was going on, although many events were still held in the auditorium, their number diminished. In fiscal 1977-78, 211 events from banquets and receptions to concerts, sporting events, and family entertainment such as the Ice Follies, the Globetrotters, and Sesame Street Live took place in the building. By fiscal 1984-85, that number had dropped to 104. Where at one time, trade shows were major users of the auditorium—the annual auto show being one of the most popular—by this time, they had almost all moved to Cal Expo or the Community Center. Many of the bands who had been able to fill the larger capacity of the auditorium in the 1960s and early 1970s had gone down in popularity and now required a smaller venue. These concerts moved to the Community Center Theater. In addition, it became more difficult for the rock promoters to get insurance, causing the number of concerts to drop off nationwide.

Nonetheless, there were a substantial number of concerts held there during the decade. The Marshall Tucker Band, Frank Zappa, Sammy Hagar, Molly Hatchet, Kenny Loggins, the Grateful Dead, Ted Nugent, the Doobie Brothers, J. Geils Band, the Tubes, Pablo Cruise, R.E.O. Speedwagon, Jimmy Buffett, Eric Clapton, and Eddie Money gave sold-out performances in the auditorium between 1977 and 1985. Willie Nelson appeared on its stage in 1979 and 1984. Boxing matches continued to be held there, as did tennis matches.

On February 5, 1986, Bill Graham Presents staged a concert in the auditorium featuring KISS and W.A.S.P. Three days later, on February 8, the roller derby ramps were set up, and the Bay Bombers clashed with the Southern Stars in Roller Derby '86. Then, dropping a bombshell, the city announced the auditorium had too many problems and would be closed immediately and indefinitely, and a task force would be appointed to determine its future. While the announcement may have come as a surprise to Sacramento residents, it was no surprise to city officials, who had stopped taking bookings for the auditorium in December.

Jackson Browne performing at the No Nukes Concert in the early 1980s (above), and Molly Hatchet on stage in 1979 (right). Greg Savalin.

By this time the number of reasons for closing the building had grown. In addition to safety deficiencies in the building and competition presented by other facilities, problems in the insurance industry had become yet another consideration. At issue was the expiration of the city's liability insurance and its fiscal inability to renew it at the greatly increased rate. Because of a legal doctrine known as the "deep pockets rule," insurance companies were declining to insure cities or were charging them unaffordable rates. The doctrine refers to situations in which parties to

lawsuits who are viewed as wealthy, such as cities and public agencies, end up having to pay a share of the damages for defendants who cannot afford them, even though the agency's responsibility in the case may have been minimal. The cost to insurance companies resulting from these cases had risen to the point where the companies could no longer afford to insure deep-pocket clients.

An incident at a concert also helped to force the city's decision. A bottle rocket set off by a concert patron hit the ceiling and sent plaster dust cascading over the audience. City officials viewed the incident with great concern, realizing the consequences could have been much greater. It was a sobering event for a city that had been holding its breath over its lack of liability insurance.

Still, it was not an easy decision for the City Council. At their meeting on February 18, all the council members agreed that something had to be done, but some felt that a way should be found to keep the building open, while others felt it should, indeed, be closed immediately. Several council members made suggestions regarding how the city might finance the renovation. Mayor Anne Rudin commented, "If everyone who walked down that aisle in a high school graduation sent in even a small amount, I think we'd have a nice nest egg with which to begin the restoration."

The Folk Dance Society, scheduled to hold its annual festival in the building on March 8 and 9, beseeched the council to keep the auditorium open until then, as there was not enough time for them to make other arrangements, and they had already had posters and pamphlets printed. Agreeing that it was unlikely that an earthquake would occur during the two-day event, they voted to close the building on March 9, at the end of the Folk Dance Festival. However, Councilman Tom Chinn admonished the folk dancers to "dance softly."

Although many Sacramentans' attention was focused on the rapidly rising rivers that would soon result in the worst floods in the Sacramento Valley since 1955, some in the community reacted immediately. Concern over the auditorium's continued existence resurfaced. Glenn Hagele, a local marketing consultant, formed an ad hoc group called Citizens to Save the Auditorium, citing the Alhambra Theater's demolition as a factor motivating his action. Hagele's concern was that the exterior be saved, regardless of what was done on the inside. Within days he received hundreds of supportive phone calls. Rumors that the building would, in fact, be torn down seemed to spreading like the flood waters, and council members and city officials were vehement in their efforts to contain them. Community Center manager Sam Burns told the *Bee*, "The first thing people tell me is

'You'll tear that building down over my dead body....'"[2] Councilman Kastanis assured the *Bee* reporter that they would not consider tearing the auditorium down, adding, "The person who even suggests such a thing will be lashed with a whip and sent to Siberia."[3]

While Hagele was challenging the city's report on the danger of the ceiling, the city's high school students, wanting to have their graduation ceremonies in the auditorium where they had been held for decades, were busy gathering signatures on petitions.

The folk dance festival was the final event before the auditorium closed for ten years. (*Owen Brewer*).

The graduations had been rescheduled for the Community Center exhibit hall, and the students were unhappy about the change. A group of thirty students handed City Council the petitions carrying 192 signatures of students from all of the city's schools. While the council members sympathized with the students, they were adamant in their refusal to allow the graduations to take place in the auditorium.

Meanwhile, the nineteen-member task force appointed to determine the auditorium's fate began its work, culling a list of over twenty suggested uses down to six. Discarded immediately were such ideas as a hospital, a school, a governor's mansion, a dinner theater, a food court, and a retail center. The six alternatives that remained under consideration after the first few meetings were to make the building a multi-purpose auditorium—as it had always been; a cultural center, with art galleries and a performing arts theater; a concert hall, designed especially for musical and dance performances with the acoustics to accommodate them; an exhibit hall, to supplement the Community Center; the central library—an idea the city librarian had already rejected; or "Smithsonian-West"—an extension of the Smithsonian Institution in Washington, D.C. with similar exhibits, an idea which the Smithsonian immediately rejected. By July 1986, the task force had narrowed the options down to two: a multi-purpose auditorium or a fixed-seat theater. The debate to decide between the two options began immediately and heated up quickly.

The city facilities management staff favored the theater plan, stressing that the Community Center Theater was so heavily booked by community groups that they were sometimes unable to accommodate road shows. Leonard Zerilli, assistant director of the Community Center, explained that a three thousand-or-so seat theater would fill a gap in Sacramento's entertainment schedule and provide a useful supplement to the Community Center Theater. By the end of 1986, the task force had concluded that a new theater was the highest and best use for the old structure. By a vote of 13-6, the task force proposed converting the auditorium into a fixed-seat performing arts theater that would complement and supplement the Community Center Theater. The fixed-seat theater plan was estimated to cost between $12 million and $15 million.

All of the task force members were not in agreement, however, and the City Council soon found itself embroiled in a controversy that pitted the veterans groups against the performing arts community. The dissenters presented a minority report arguing that the conversion would detract from the memorial aspect of the building, destroy some of its unique and special features, reduce the seating capacity, increase

ticket prices, and make the building generally less accessible to Sacramentans. With issues ranging from the condition of the ceiling to the comparative cost of one scheme over the other, tense exchanges at council meetings throughout the winter months heated the chambers. The perceived need to replace the ceiling with a fiberglass replica was one of the items that caused the price tag on the retention of the auditorium to exceed that of creating a fixed-seat theater, eliminating much of the existing ceiling. In January, Councilman Tom Chinn suggested taking the issue to the voters along with a financing proposal. It would be years before that happened.

You Can't Hear Anything In That Big Barn

Mention the acoustics in the Memorial Auditorium and you are liable to get a strongly worded response. The auditorium, sometimes referred to as "that big barn," has had acoustical problems throughout its existence. The ability to hear clearly in the building has long been a source of complaints. Oddly though, not everyone has agreed with the criticism.

Unquestionably, acoustics in such a large space present a substantial challenge. At the time the auditorium was designed and built, the science of architectural acoustics was in its infancy. Acoustical treatment had been previously, and still was to a great extent, based on precedent: what had seemed to work in the past.

During the design phase, the city retained an acoustical expert to review the plans. The expert reported that he found the design of the wall and ceiling curves to be correct. When the room was filled with people, the acoustics would be nearly perfect. He suggested using sound-deadening plaster to aid the acoustics when the room was only partially filled. Plaster that absorbs sound was used under and over the balcony and in the halls of the building. The ceiling was pierced for ventilation, and the designers thought that the web of ventilators would also aid in absorbing noise overhead.

With the grand opening of the building, the acoustics had been put to the test and had passed. All had apparently heard the speakers and the music very satisfactorily. The first performance scheduled for the building was grand opera, and there is no record of complaints; maybe everyone was still too awed by the structure to notice if they couldn't hear well. But then too, the hall was packed to capacity.

As the architects had predicted, in a packed house the acoustics performed well, but when there were smaller groups it was another matter. There must have been some complaints before the first year was over: In June a curtain was installed along the ceiling that could shut off the upper balcony and improve the acoustics for smaller gatherings.

Still there were problems. By 1936, James Dean, the building's architect, had become Sacramento's City Manager. Many complaints about the acoustics had apparently been directed to him or had been passed on to him from the auditorium management. These must have been somewhat of an affront to Dean. After widespread criticism of the acoustics following a play in the building, he banned further dramatic productions in the auditorium. The booking agents had been told that the acoustics would not support drama, but they continued to book plays. Dean said that doing so was not fair to the public or the actors and "brings unwarranted criticism upon the city."

Ten years later, the auditorium closed for two months in the summer while changes were made to improve the acoustics. Ornamental plaster grills, covered with expanded mica for sound absorption, were installed on the main ceiling, and the ceiling over the upper balconies was given an acoustical treatment.

In 1941 the issue resurfaced. The Sacramento Symphony gave some performances in the Memorial Auditorium and some at the Sacramento High School auditorium. Those held at Sacramento High had far greater richness, quality, and balance of sound, according to an editorial in the Bee. The editorial writer proposed that a shell be constructed in the auditorium to project the sound to the front of the house. Leopold Stokowski was scheduled to appear and carried his own shell; this would give the audience, and city officials, an idea of the improvement that such a device could make. It was something the editorial writer felt the city should build for the local concert goers and the players, but there is no evidence that it was ever done.

The next time the subject was publicly discussed, an organized movement formed to petition the City Council to solve the problem. The group, organized in 1952 by the Sacramento Saturday Club, was interested in the acoustics for musical performances, and again a shell was mentioned. The Sacramento Choral Society, the Philharmonic Association, the Opera Guild, and the Symphony League were also solicited to join the effort. Nearly two years later Elmer Congdon, the auditorium's manager, said he realized the problems, but there really was not much they could do about it. He pointed out that the building was an auditorium, not a concert hall or an opera house, and not a good place to see a play or musical performance. It was great for some things, and wrong for others.

In 1955, a new sound system was installed that was expected to correct the problem. The salesman from the sound equipment company was on hand for the test. He said they found that the auditorium had "...no serious acoustical problems. It simply took a knowledge of how to put the right equipment together properly."[1] All present for the test gave their approval. However, apparently the complaints persisted.

Speaking in support of a proposed community center and concert hall in 1966, City Manager Fairbairn told a symphony audience in Memorial Auditorium the "secret" of the poor acoustics. His explanation was that the ventilating holes in the ceiling were the problem. He said some of the sound produced on stage went up into the holes, rattled around in the attic and then some came back down again. Flat trays of sound reflecting material had been installed long ago, but they had to be far enough apart for the ventilation system to function, so they were never "100 percent effective." He added that the trays were still there, "doing the best they can, but some of those offbeat sounds still return to the auditorium."[2]

While the symphony-goers complained, however, other concert patrons had fewer problems with the acoustics. The numerous rock bands that played in the auditorium in the '60s and '70s seemingly had no complaints. Their enthusiastic audiences stomped on the floor creating a thunderous noise, while the bands' ear-shattering sounds did just fine rattling around in the "big old barn."

When the Community Center Theater was completed in 1974, the symphony, ballet, and opera moved into it, and the complaints lingered only in the collective memory. The fact is, the auditorium is a big barn, a wonderful, exquisite big barn. It's a great place for all sorts of things, but sometimes not for acoustically sensitive events. However, if you ever have a chance to be in the building when it's empty, try standing on the stage and having a friend go up to the balcony. You will find that you can easily carry on a conversation in a normal speaking voice and hear and be heard perfectly.

Ban Ali Shrine
Homer X Blaghe Party
May 15 1906

AUDITORIUM

ALBUM

Many of the types of events that took place in the auditorium cannot be placed within specific decades, as they were ongoing, spanning many decades. These events are recorded in this album.

Japanese Dancers at the Camellia Festival, March 1962. Tom Myers.

Paula Boghosian Collection.

Bonnie Snyder Collection.

Desert Song (right) was one of many popular musicals that graced the auditorium stage. *Courtesy of Andy Flink.*

The September Spectacular (far right) featured numerous acts and brought together both local and imported talent. *Courtesy of Fred Vail.*

The Sacramento Ballet (below) played the auditorium until the Community Center Theater was built. *Sacramento Archives and Museum Collection Center.*

THE SACRAMENTO BALLET COMPANY

Presents

an

Evening of

Ballet

WITH

Symphony Orchestra

FRITZ BERENS

CONDUCTING

Sacramento Memorial Auditorium

March 22, 1958

SKATING *Vanities* of 1951

Souvenir Program Twenty Five Cents

Performances such as the Strauss Festival (above) were popular events, especially in the early years. *Courtesy of Cal and Hilda Kerfoot.*

In the 1960s-1980s concerts such as this country music program (left) were the main attractions. *Courtesy of Fred Vail.*

The Skating Vanities (right), performing on roller skates, were regulars for many years. *Courtesy of Dottie Graves.*

The Gay and Lilting Melodies of

STRAUSS FESTIVAL

JOHANN STRAUSS • JOSEPH STRAUSS • OSCAR STRAUS

in a

with

OSCAR STRAUS

Composer of "THE CHOCOLATE SOLDIER"

in Person

Assistant Conductor
ERWIN STRAUS

SOLOISTS • CONCERT ORCHESTRA

Wed., OCTOBER 30, 1946
8:30 P.M.

SACRAMENTO AUDITORIUM

Prices: $3.60, $3.00, $2.40, $1.80, $1.20 (incl. tax)
Tickets on Sale: Ware-Hazelton Box Office,
Weinstock Lubin Co.
Mail Orders now: Ware-Hazelton Box Office,
Weinstock Lubin Co.

A CONCERT THEATRE, LTD. PRESENTATION

KRAK Radio presents

"IN PERSON"

COUNTRY MUSIC

BLOCKBUSTER

JOHNNY CASH
and The TENNESSEE THREE

GEORGE JONES
and The Jones Boys

FARON YOUNG

FLATT & SCRUGGS

GRANDPA JONES

MOTHER MAYBELLE
and the CARTER FAMILY

JUNE CARTER

QUARTET

PLAINSMEN
LORETTA LYNN ★ GEORGIE RIDDLE

Produced by SAUL HOLIZ

SUN. JUNE 23
2 SHOWS 2 P.M. and 8 P.M.

MEMORIAL AUD.

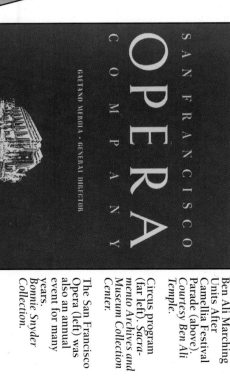

Ben Ali Marching Units After Camellia Festival Parade (above). Courtesy Ben Ali Temple.

Circus program (far left). Sacramento Archives and Museum Collection Center.

The San Francisco Opera (left) was also an annual event for many years. Bonnie Snyder Collection.

Round One!

The auditorium served as the principal boxing venue for the Sacramento region from its opening match on March 3, 1927, until the building's closure in 1986. The availability of an arena seating more than 4,000 for the use of the sport helped make Sacramento a center not only for the staging of matches but also for the training and discovery of new talent as well. The existence of this site encouraged the generation of a boxing industry in Sacramento, attracting youths, gyms for training them, boxing managers, fight promoters, and a sizable and loyal constituency of fans. "Boxing night" at the auditorium was generally on Tuesdays, while wrestling matches appeared every Monday night.

Gyms and small arenas often generated rivalries which promoters then booked as matches for the auditorium's larger audience. One of the largest auditorium audiences of 4,619 fans viewed a bout between Lloyd Marshall and "Newsboy" Millich on May Day of 1942. Marshall also took a ten-round decision over "Newsboy's" brother, George Millich, whom he fought in 1948. Marshall won kudos from a core group of longtime fight fans and promoters as perhaps the city's all-time best boxer. Not all of the arena fighters were as popular, however. In May 1948 the *Sacramento Bee* wrote:

Last night's bouts were with the new precautionary eight ounce gloves, and under the eight count rule for all knockdowns or knockouts. However, there were no knockdowns or knockouts. That was not due to the larger gloves but because most of the fighters could not have knocked down anybody if they had a sledge hammer in one hand and an atomic bomb in the other.

Over time, several local "headliners" gained notoriety through the auditorium fights. Besides Lloyd Marshall, other popular fighters in the 1930s-1940s included the three Romero brothers, Elwood, Jackie, and "Tomboy." Joey Lopes rose to regional acclaim in the 1950s, ultimately fighting world champion Joe Brown three times. In the 1960s, Bill McMurray became prominent, fighting all the big names of the era: Sonny Liston, Floyd Patterson, Ken Norton, Eddie Machen, and Boone Kirkman. Pete Ranzany became a top professional in the 1970s and a number-one contender in an era of top welterweights that saw the likes of Sugar Ray Leonard, Tommy Hearns, and Pipino Cuevas. In the 1980s, Bobby Chacon, two-time world champion, entered his second successful decade as a junior lightweight. Auditorium boxing fans would chant, "Bob-bee, Bob-bee," to encourage the popular fighter to victory. *Ring* magazine voted his 1982 bout with "Bazooka" Limon at the

Boxer Bobby Chacon weighing in at the auditorium before a fight.
Dennis Warren.

Collegiate boxing tournament at the auditorium.
Sacramento Archives and Museum Collection Center.

Pete Ranzany fought Wilfredo Benitez at the auditorium in 1976. *Courtesy of Stan Bollinger.*

DRESS CIRCLE
SEC ROW SEAT
16 F 2

PROFESSIONAL BOXING
SACRAMENTO MEMORIAL AUDITORIUM
SACRAMENTO, CA
TUESDAY 8:00 P.M.

$10.00
DRESS CIRCLE
SEC ROW SEAT
12 A 10

auditorium as its Fight of the Year. Chacon helped teach his one-time sparring partner, Tony Lopez, how to fight. He did such a good job that Lopez went on to become junior lightweight world champion.

Out of five fights noted as all-time, unforgettable landmarks of the Sacramento fight scene, four took place in the Memorial Auditorium. The fifth took place at Arco Arena, after the closure of the auditorium.

Longtime boxing fans and professionals alike have special feelings about the fights held at the auditorium. The ambiance there is perfect for the events, and the lower balcony seats are the best anywhere for visibility. In the old days, local promoters would arrange places for out-of-town contenders to stay in the

auditorium's neighborhood. After the fights, everyone would repair to Georgian's restaurant at 19th and J Streets for a snack. "Pidge" ran the kitchen at Georgian's and was a boxing fan himself; the after-boxing atmosphere there was that of a large family.

The auditorium arena was also the chosen venue for both college title fights like the Pacific Coast Intercollegiate and National Intercollegiate championships and for sub-regional trials for the U.S. Olympic boxing team in 1948. In 1940 Ted Kara, whose record included winning twenty college matches without a defeat and service as a member of the 1936 U.S. Olympic boxing team, headed the college boxing team.

Sacramento's best-known fight manager and a foremost figure of the professional boxing world in the 1930s and 1940s was Ancil Hoffman, who managed Max Baer and Buddy Baer. A local pioneer of the sport, he did much to set the stage for the growth of boxing in this region. Ancil got his start in sports wearing a wig and playing third base on the Boston Bloomer Girls baseball team. He later became a lightweight boxer of note back when "putting horseshoes inside the gloves was considered mild treatment."[1] He once told the Bee, "It is a wonderful thing to have the amateur boxing trials in Sacramento....Amateur boxing does things for young men....It develops their bodies and character. The college boxing held in Sacramento each year is one of the greatest events I ever have witnessed."[2]

For amateurs and professionals, boxing was (and still is) big in Sacramento, and the Memorial Auditorium has always played a big role in the city's love affair with the sport.

Billie Jean King played tennis in the auditorium during a celebrity tennis tournament.
Courtesy of Rich LaVoie.

The Harlem Globetrotters came to the Memorial Auditorium annually in January.
Sacramento Bee.

WRESTLING

Wrestling matches were the regular Monday night event at the auditorium. When Lanette Franklin was about nine, her father and her grandfather took her to see a match there. She had never been before, and her most vivid memory is of everyone repeatedly shouting "choke." Since they were sitting quite a distance from the ring, her grandfather yelled it very loudly. It seemed a very odd thing to the little girl, until she found out it meant that one wrestler was choking the other and the crowd was making sure the referee knew it.

Courtesy of Ron Green, Sacramento Convention Center.

"They Used to Let Us Out of School for the Circus"

A baby elephant gets a hosing off before going into the arena. *Sacramento Bee Collection (Dick Schmidt). Sacramento Archives and Museum Collection Center.*

Nearly everyone over twenty-five who grew up in Sacramento remembers the circus at the Memorial Auditorium. The Shrine/Polack Bros. Circus was an annual event there every May from 1935 to 1986. One of the best parts was the fact that the schools actually gave students the afternoon off to attend.

The circus was sponsored by the Ben Ali Shrine Temple. It was both their annual fund-raiser for the temple's operating expenses and their community project. Members sold tickets to provide funds for the temple, but tickets were also given out free to underprivileged and orphaned children. After the auditorium closed in 1986, the circus moved elsewhere. It presently appears annually in Folsom, still sponsored by Ben Ali Temple.

The opening of the circus was preceded by the Shrine parade. No circus members participated in the parade; they were busy setting up the circus. But all of the Shrine units were represented: marching units, motorcycle units, marching bands, and Shrine clowns. The parade ended in front of the auditorium, where everyone assembled for photos. Some units also marched into the arena at the beginning of the circus performance.

Arriving in Sacramento by train, the circus continued to the auditorium on foot or in wagons. Once there, the circus wagons and campers lined up along the perimeter of the block, and began the job of preparing for the event. Stage hands from Local 50 of the International Alliance of Theatrical Stage Employees (IATSE) did the rigging for the trapeze performances. Walking on 2' x 12' boards laying across the rafters over the suspended plaster ceiling, they dropped the rigging

through removable ceiling medallions and secured it to the pipe rails along the balcony. They also had to call in the Montgomery House Moving Company to reinforce the floor so it could support the weight of the animals.

Some of the animals stayed in the basement, where the elephants left damaged posts and a broken organ flue as permanent testimony to their occupation. The elephants were brought from the basement to the main floor one by one in the huge freight elevator. While it was a hassle for the circus crew, the elevator carried the elephants without a problem.

Animals residing in the basement also had other consequences. John Cox, son of longtime stage manager Francis Cox and later stage manager himself for many years, remembers earning good money as a teenager when the circus was in town. The elephant and cat waste was continuously shoveled up and loaded onto a flatbed trailer parked in the basement. There was a lot of waste and the trailer was not very big. So, John's job was to hitch up the trailer each morning before school and each evening after school, drive it to the city dump, unload it, and return it to the basement. He earned $75 for the week.

The thing that set Polack Bros. Circus apart from all others was that it used buildings rather than tents. Polack Bros. was a pioneer of this idea, which came about, in part, because circuses were so dependent on the weather. Some performers

The bear on the bicycle (above) mimics the program cover illustration. Rope supports for trapeze swings (right) come through the ceiling. So apparently, did the artists. *Sacramento Bee Collection, Sacramento Archives and Museum Collection Center.*

would work the tent shows in the summer, then go with Polack in winter. Soon Ringling Bros. followed Polack Bros.' lead and also began working in buildings.

The Polack Bros. performers liked working in the auditorium because of its beauty and because of the beautiful foyer. They liked the foyer because it was a great place for their sales items and they always did very well with them there. They didn't like setting up at the auditorium, however, because it was hot up in the ceiling area where the rigging was attached. Nor did they like having to drag their trunks up and down all those stairs to the dressing rooms. In addition, parking was limited around the building, and they could not get their trailers and campers as close as they would have liked.

They loved Sacramento, though, because Sam's Hofbrau, with the beef roasts and turkeys turning on spits in the window, was just down the street. The circus manager used to make a deal with Sam's to keep the Hofbrau open late a couple of nights. Then the whole crew would

walk to the restaurant and have a big feast after they closed the circus down. Sometimes on those nights the audience would not get the usual music played as they left, because the band and the performers were in such a hurry to get over to Sam's.

A Special Memory

The Memorial Auditorium has an extra special place in Neil Calmes' heart because his very first job was there. When he was just twelve years old, he, his older brother, and a friend of his brother's were hanging around the auditorium watching the circus set up. One of the managers spotted them and asked the older boys if they would like a job. They said they would and were made clowns for the clown walk. Neil said he wanted to be a clown too, but the manager told him he was too young. After the manager was unable to find anyone else for the part and Neil repeated his request a couple more times, the manager relented and allowed the youngster to participate.

He was given the costume of an ostrich that had a big head, a neck that turned, and a monkey on its back that covered Neil's head. The costume was difficult to manage; he had to be helped in and out of it and had trouble seeing out of the peep hole, but he didn't give up. Although he occasionally took a wrong turn, Neil felt good about his performance. His favorite part, however, was all the young girls who gathered by the stage door clamoring for his autograph. Needless to say, he proudly signed their programs.

Bethel Temple, now Capital Christian Center, held an annual Singing Christmas Tree at the auditorium. *Courtesy of Capital Christian Center.*

Preparations for the Ice Follies. *Sacramento Bee.*

Ice Follies at the auditorium in 1978. All 27 performances that year were sold out. *Sacramento Bee.*

Ice Shows

Ice shows came to the auditorium annually; they were one of the most popular events. The Ice Capades was one. The Ice Capades skaters enjoyed performing in the auditorium because they were so close to the audience there, unlike many of the other buildings in which they performed.

But how did the arena floor get turned into an ice rink? The ice shows had two sets of their own equipment: One set they sent to the next city on their schedule while they skated on the other. Stagehands from Local 50 of IATSE and various tradesmen would help install it. The stagehands put edges along the perimeter and covered the floor with plastic fabric; plumbers assembled refrigeration pipes over the floor; then workers brought in sawdust by the wheelbarrowful and covered the pipes. When all was ready, the area was filled with brine and frozen. The process took several days. When the show was over, workers broke the ice up with sledge hammers and hauled it out to the street in the wheelbarrows. Then the assembly process was reversed.

Another special accommodation the auditorium staff made for the ice shows was to set up tables of sewing machines in the basement. With so many elaborate costumes, the ice shows had seamstresses on staff who altered, repaired, and mended the garments regularly.

136

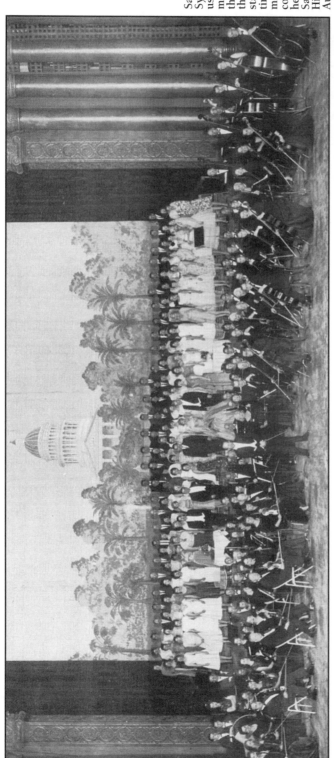

Sacramento Symphony, 1962, using one of the many backdrops that hung above the auditorium stage. By this time, however, most of the concerts were held in the Sacramento High School Auditorium.

Sacramento Bee Collection (Leo Neibaur), Sacramento Archives and Museum Collection Center.

All Those Elephants

The late Georgia Berry, for many years director of St. Albans School, never really liked the auditorium much. She said it was "all those elephants" that bothered her. "You could go to the circus one day and the next night hear a concert, in the same place the elephants had been the day before." It just didn't seem quite right to Georgia. But she wasn't the only one so bothered. Longtime Sacramento Celebrity Series and A.M. Series manager Wilma Lewis once had to schedule virtuoso violinist Isaac Stern into the auditorium the night before the circus, with the elephants already

ensconced in the basement. Because of their trumpeting, all but one of the elephants were moved to a nearby vacant lot before the concert. Left inside on the wintry night was a baby elephant with a cold. Lewis held her breath during the concert, knowing that the sick elephant was right below Stern. Right in the middle of a beautiful cadenza, Lewis heard a sad little trumpet, in the same key as the piece. She did not know whether Stern heard it or not, but she couldn't help thinking that the little pachyderm had very good taste.

Annual events for children were the Christmas shows put on by various groups. Campbell Soup brought Timmie and Lassie to entertain the children of their employees one year. In this photo of the Sacramento Bee's Christmas Show in 1943, lights from the projection booth illuminate the stage. *Sacramento Bee Collection, Sacramento Archives and Museum Collection Center.*

Dogs and pony on stage in 1969 (below left). *Sacramento Bee Collection (Dick Schmidt) Sacramento Archives and Museum Collection Center.*

Santa visits with youngsters, 1962. *Sacramento Bee.*

An eager audience watches the Bee Christmas Show. *Sacramento Bee.*

140

The Sacramento Ballet gave their performances in the auditorium until the Community Center Theater opened in 1974. Here, the ballet performs *Paquita* at the auditorium.
Courtesy of Barbara Crockett, Sacramento Ballet.

Formerly with the Sacramento Ballet, Deborah Dobson dances in the *Nutcracker* as a visiting ballerina from the American Ballet Theater.
Courtesy of Barbara Crockett, Sacramento Ballet.

The annual Piano Festivals held in the auditorium began in 1959. The piano teachers all taught their students the same duets. At the festival, the young pianists played the pieces simultaneously, accompanied by the auditorium organ and directed by symphony conductor, Fritz Berens. What a thrilling sound that must have been to those proud parents. In 1963 Anne Rudin's daughter participated in the festival. The mother and daughter played the duet together in their home for many years afterward. *Courtesy of Wally Clark.*

Bill Rase's Orchestra, shown here in 1965, was one of many local groups that played for dances and proms in the auditorium over the years. *Courtesy of Bill Rase.*

FRITZ BERENS, Conductor

SACRAMENTO PIANO FESTIVAL

IRENE JAMES, Chairman

SIRUS STUDIO

Second Annual

Sacramento Piano Festival

1500 Pianists

Program

110 Pianos

SUNDAY MAY 22, 1960   2:00 P.M. and 4:00 P.M.

SACRAMENTO MEMORIAL AUDITORIUM

BALDWIN PIANOS from FLEMING MUSIC CO.

The First Methodist Church held Easter services in the auditorium for many years. Each of the church's choirs performed. The youth choirs had to arrive early and wait their turn. Ruth McCreary and Else Meyer were two of the women whose duty it was to oversee the youngsters over the years. Governor Earl Warren attended the services regularly. Paschel Monk, Professor of Music at Sacramento State University, was Choir Director at the time this photo was taken. Dr. A. Raymond Grant was the minister from 1946–1974 and was also on the board of the Community Concert Series. Jean Salmon, Dr. Grant's daughter, remembers getting to go backstage to meet Marian Anderson. *Sacramento Archives and Museum Collection Center.*

SACRAMENTO SENIOR HIGH SCHOOL

CLASSES OF 1951

Presents

The Annual
Senior Ball

&

SATURDAY, JANUARY 13, 1951

BILL RASES' ORCHESTRA

Memorial Auditorium   *Eight to Twelve*

Courtesy of Bill Rase.

Sacramento High
School prom, 1958.
Courtesy of Annette Deglow.

TENTH ANNUAL
COMMENCEMENT

SACRAMENTO
JUNIOR COLLEGE

Wednesday evening, May Twenty-eighth
Nineteen hundred and thirty
at eight o'clock

SACRAMENTO MEMORIAL AUDITORIUM

Most everyone who went to high school in Sacramento remembers graduation at the auditorium. Sacramento Junior College, before it became Sacramento City College, also held graduation in the building, as this program from 1930 (left) attests. The Sacramento High School graduation of 1962 started by picking up gowns in the basement (above). A commencement speaker addresses her classmates from the podium on stage (right).

Candlebearers who lighted the way for the graduates exit behind them (left). Commencement speakers await their turns on the stage (above). A graduate receives her diploma (right). *Courtesy of Dennis Warren.*

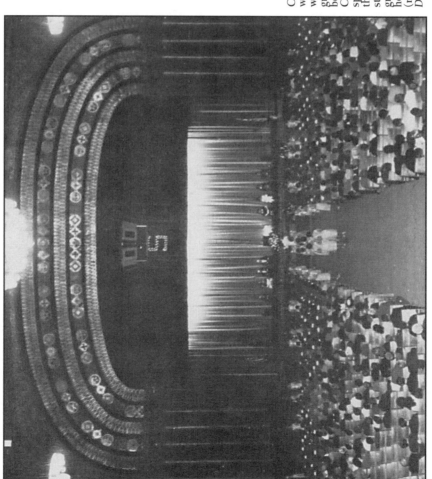

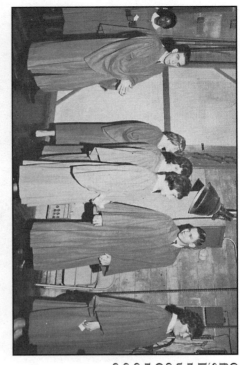

Graduating seniors from Sacramento High School's class of '63 line up in the auditorium basement to pick up their actual diplomas (left). Graduates of Sacramento High School's class of '38 gather outside after the ceremony (below left).

The veterans' organizations were frequent users of the auditorium for conventions and meetings of various kinds. Here, Ken Robbins is installed as Junior Vice Commander of the California Veterans of Foriegn Wars. *Courtesy of Ken Robbins.*

Decade Seven: 1987 - 1997

The Dark Years

A lthough plans for the future use of the auditorium were frequently in the news as the decade turned, on February 22, 1987, not a soul noted the sixtieth anniversary of its opening. The city's and the country's attention was focused on the newly revealed Iran-Contra affair, in which profits from sales of arms to Iran were covertly diverted to the Contra rebels in Nicaragua, bypassing a Congressional ban on giving them aid. In the Sacramento City Council chambers, the debates that had taken place over the auditorium's fate had been resolved, but before the decade was over, many more were to come. The building that had been the source of so much controversy during its original planning and construction, and throughout the following six decades, was now the source of more disputes, even as it sat dark and vacant.

Although the means for financing it was still undetermined, City Council approved the task force's proposal in May 1987, and appointed the Auditorium Design Advisory Committee to work with city staff and the consultants, Vitiello and Associates, to help with the design of the fixed-seat theater. One year later the design advisory committee released an architectural programming study spelling out what was to be included in the conversion. While the debates

of the previous year had indicated that the new theater would have a capacity of over 3,000, the study specified a 2,750 seat facility, about 350 more seats than the Community Center Theater. The exterior of the building would remain unaltered as had been promised, except for the rear where storage and a new loading dock were proposed. Two methods of providing for these items were put forth: One would move the stage forward to make room for the storage and loading areas; the other would construct a bubble that would protrude over the I Street sidewalk and parking lane. To mollify the veterans' objections, the plan also included erecting a veterans' memorial in front of the building.

As the year ended, the city hired a project team consisting of Polshek and Partners of New York and local firm Dreyfuss and Blackford. The Polshek firm had just completed a much-touted renovation of Carnegie Hall: They were an excellent selection. With the design underway, the city faced the financing issue. The auditorium was not the only project in the hopper. The expansion of the Community Center had been discussed and planned for many years. There were others, too. The city went to the voters with a bond measure that incorporated funds for five projects in all. While a few years before, $12-15 mil-

The interior of the Memorial Auditorium transposed into a fixed-seat theater according to the design of James Stewart Polshek and Partners; Dreyfuss and Blackford Architects, and 3Di, Inc.

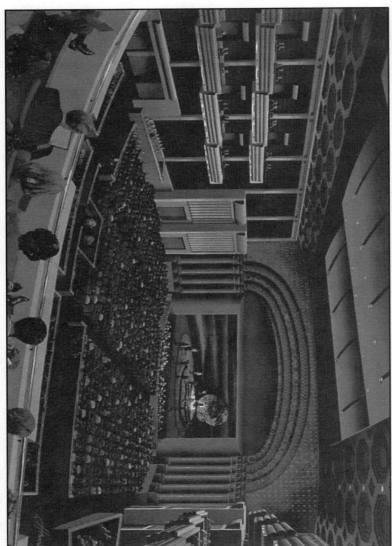

lion had been the estimated cost for converting the auditorium into a theater, $38 million of the measure's funds were allocated to the project. In early 1991, the design team unveiled their preliminary plans to an expectant city.

Although the city felt that it was retaining a considerable amount of the building's historic fabric, what was unveiled was a beautiful theater that removed a large portion of the ceiling and replaced it with acoustical panels and sound equipment, pulled the walls in, taking out the balconies, adding boxes, and reducing the seating capacity to 2,500—down to just 50 seats more than the Community Center Theater. What Sacramento would now have was two theaters of almost exactly the same capacity, designed to accommodate the same kinds of events. From a booking standpoint this was not what had been intended. Unfortunately, having spent $5 million on the plans, the city was hardly in a position to turn back now.

Sitting in his living room reading the newspaper one evening shortly after the plans were released, Richard La Voie got his first glimpse of published renderings of the conversion. His heart sank. As a preservationist, Rich had had serious concerns about turning the building into a theater, but he never guessed what it would really mean to the structure until that moment. Unable to sleep that night, Rich resolved that something had to be done. At the time, he envisioned writing letters to city council members and newspaper editors. Talks with other preservationists, however, led to a meeting at a local restaurant.

Open wounds from previous fights began to bleed again, as they reviewed the recently lost battle to save the Merrium Apartments, slated for demolition as part of the Convention Center expansion project. They became determined to save the auditorium.

beautiful interior from meeting a similar fate. Just as the original controversy over the building's site had re-erupted while the plans were being drawn in 1925, now with the new drawings completed, the issue of what to do with the aging structure resurfaced. More controversy was on the way; history was repeating itself.

The board of the Sacramento Old City Association (SOCA), which included two members of the auditorium task force who had favored the theater scheme, was supportive of the city's plans. One of the first moves of the new group would have to be to get SOCA's board to reverse their position. Rich arranged with the city facilities management staff for a tour of the building for SOCA members on March 18. Thinking he meant the twelve or so members of the board, the city officials agreed. Over one hundred people, most of whom were avid preservationists, showed up at the auditorium that stormy night. The officials were astounded and annoyed but proceeded with the tour, explaining all of the proposed alterations. The assembled group was appalled; none had realized the extent of the destruction that was planned. After the tour, the group met at the Fort Sutter Post of the American Legion to discuss the matter. At the end of the meeting a vote was taken to rescind the organization's endorsement of the city's plan. The vote was nearly unanimous.

However, winning over the SOCA membership did not win over the board, which declined to follow through on the members' vote. But with a body of support established, Councilman Josh Pane suggested that the council reverse their decision. In April, Polshek's representatives came from New York and made a formal presentation of the construction documents to City Council. The opposition presented itself in the form of intensive questioning from Pane, and once again the air heated up in the council chambers. The opposition committee was on hand, but time precluded their testimony. The issue was continued until the next meeting.

The following week, the group, including a SOCA board member who had served on the task force, testified before the council. In response, several councilmembers displayed open hostility to the group's suggestions. It was an acrimonious afternoon that foreshadowed future debates on the matter. At the end of the day, the council approved the documents.

THE FATE OF MEMORIAL AUDITORIUM

will be discussed at a public forum MONDAY, MARCH 18, 7:00 to 9:00 P.M. at the Fort Sutter Post of the American Legion, 1119 21st Street. The meeting is sponsored by the Sacramento Old City Association.

This is one of the city's most important landmarks! Should it remain a multi-purpose auditorium, or should the city turn it into a theater? Come and share your views!

Courtesy of Richard La Voie.

Courtesy of Rich LaVoie

The City Attorney of the City of Sacramento has prepared the following title and summary of the chief purpose and points of the proposed measure:

INITIATIVE MEASURE TO BE SUBMITTED DIRECTLY TO THE VOTERS

AN INITIATIVE ORDINANCE REGULATING THE PRESERVATION, REHABILITATION AND OPERATION OF THE SACRAMENTO MEMORIAL AUDITORIUM AS A MULTI-PURPOSE ARENA

This initiative measure, which is a proposed ordinance, would require that the Sacramento Memorial Auditorium, located on J and 15th Streets, 16th Street, 'J' Street, and 'I' Street, be preserved, maintained, and operated in its original form and configuration as a multi-purpose arena-style facility, consistent with the United States' Secretary of the Interior's Standards for Rehabilitation and Guidelines for Rehabilitating Historic Building' (1990 revision), and the State Historic Safety Code Sections 18950, et seq., and regulations which require the City Council to rehabilitate and restore the Auditorium...

NOTICE TO THE PUBLIC: THIS PETITION MAY BE CIRCULATED BY A PAID SIGNATURE-GATHERER OR A VOLUNTEER. YOU HAVE THE RIGHT TO ASK.

If adopted, the proposed ordinance could not be repealed or amended except by majority vote of the voters of the City of Sacramento.

DECLARATION OF CIRCULATOR (To be completed after above signatures have been obtained.)

INSTRUCTIONS TO PETITION CIRCULATOR

Save The Auditorium! 310 - 25th Street, Sacramento, CA 95816 (916) 447-0909.

Once the group saw that their entreaties had done nothing to change the council's mind, they realized that they would have to take more drastic steps. The group prepared a lawsuit to bring against the city and began working on an initiative to put before the voters. Meanwhile the city prepared to proceed with the first task toward the implementation of their project: that of removing the asbestos from the building. Fearing that the asbestos removal would lead to extensive demolition, the opposition group returned to inform the council of their intentions and request that the removal be postponed or that the contractor be required to keep the damage to a minimum. Their requests met with more rancor and, once again, accomplished nothing.

While the asbestos came off the walls of the building, the group legitimized themselves, decided on a name—"Save the Auditorium!" (STA!)—and Richard La Voie set about polishing the draft ballot initiative he had written. At 10:00 on the morning of July 3, 1991, after weeks of discussion, revisions, and review, "Save the Auditorium!" filed the initiative with the City Clerk. That afternoon, with their spirits as high as the flags they waved, STA! held a press conference on the building's front steps. Two weeks later the initiative was certified by the city clerk and "Save the Auditorium!" took to the streets to collect the approximately twenty-nine thousand needed signatures. Within a month and a half, it became clear that this could not be done by volunteers. The Sacramento Old City Association board, which had suffered some resignations over the issue, but had continued to withhold support, finally relented and provided money to hire professional petition circulators to supplement the group's effort.

In January 1992, STA! turned in over thirty-three thousand signatures to be checked and verified by the City Clerk. Late on a Friday afternoon in early February, word came that the initiative had qualified and would appear on the ballot as Measure H. STA! felt confident that their work was over, and victory was theirs.

Councilman Josh Pane and Richard LaVoie at rally announcing success of signature campaign (top). World War I veterans at Measure H rally on the steps of the auditorium on Armed Forces Day, 1992 (above). *Courtesy of Richard La Voie.*

In fact, the war had just begun. In the coming months and throughout the summer, STA! found themselves in an intense battle against the city and key members of the performing arts community. Josh Pane, running for mayor, closely allied himself with the measure, using it as a campaign issue. Mayor Anne Rudin, who had long thought Sacramento needed another theater to accommodate the cultural direction in which she saw the city growing, had visions of the auditorium becoming a grand concert hall. She and the other proponents of the theater project organized into a group they called SMART (Sacramentans for Memorial Auditorium Renovation, Tommorrow) and launched a "No on Measure H" campaign in rebuttal. Both sides hired campaign firms and engaged in all the feats of political warfare they could manage, including the obligatory hurling of accusations.

The STA! campaign staged three rallies, two of which were disastrous failures. The kick-off event held on May 1, 1992, a Friday afternoon two days after the riots in Los Angeles, and the day of a shooting in a school near Marysville, failed to get much of a turnout. The radio mobile broadcasting truck crew and the attending STA! members listened alone to a band they did not enjoy. In addition, the execution of Robert Alton Harris upstaged what had been planned as a dramatic press conference on the steps of City Hall. Only a single reporter attended.

At the close of election day, with over eighty-four thousand votes cast and several hundred absentee ballots left to be counted, Measure H had only a ninety-nine vote margin of victory. The absentee ballots could, in fact, change the results. Two weeks later, at about 6:30 in the evening, Richard La Voie and several other members of the STA! team drove out to the Bradshaw Road office of the Registrar of Voters to get the final results. They learned that their margin of victory had actually gone up; they had won by 221 votes.

Because of the strong emotions connected with the issue, recriminations were inevitable. Some wanted to try again, putting both plans side by side on the ballot. Instead, Mayor Rudin appointed the fifteen-member Citizens' Advisory Committee (CAC) called for in Measure H, and planning for the building's future look began anew.

The committee appointees turned out to be nearly evenly divided between people who favored the theater plan and people associated with Measure H. These two camps, aligning themselves on opposite sides of a large meeting room table, would have to try to reach some kind of consensus.

During the campaign, the Measure H proponents had claimed that they would save the city $20 million of the $40 million allocated to the project in the bond issue. However, when the committee came together, it was unclear to the members how much money they would have for the project. Mayor Rudin told the committee that the money was not their concern, and at her request, they began planning three levels of work from a "dream scheme" to a bargain-basement version. Nonetheless, when city staff presented the schemes to city council with the request for funds to be released to hire a cost-estimating consultant, the council was unwilling to give over funds. One councilman asked, "What is the least amount of money needed just to get the doors opened?"

The city was suffering from economic problems. The Community Center expansion had gone over its budget; hotel tax revenues had not met the city's estimates; and Sacramento was in an austerity mode. The councilman was literally asking for the cost of meeting minimal code requirements: boarding up the stairs; if necessary, taking out the ceiling and not replacing it; sweeping the floors; cleaning the restrooms; and buying new locks. The committee learned that virtually none of the money from the bond issue would now be available for the project. In the end, the rehabilitation would have to be completed with just $10.8 million from the Sacramento Housing and Redevelopment agency and residual bond funds.

Over the course of many months, the committee, working with city staff from the Facilities Management and Architectural and Engineering Departments, managed to define a scope of work—taken from the pared-down version of their plan—that they felt could be accomplished within the budget now available. Unfortunately, the greatest part of the budget would be taken up with the seismic repairs to the building. Little would be available for other, more visible improvements. Although they had originally planned to hire an architect to draw up the plans, the city suggested that it would be more efficient and economical to abandon usual method of approaching a job, wherein the client tells the architect what they want, the architect produces a design that fulfills the requirements and contractors bid on the job,

MEASURE H

Failing to convince the City Council to reconsider their plans to change the Memorial Auditorium into a fixed-seat theater, the Save The Auditorium! committee wrote an initiative to present to the voters. The initiative, known as Measure H, outlined the importance of the building to the city and its citizens and called for it to be "preserved, maintained and operated by the City in its original form and configuration as a multi-use, arena-style facility." The authors included two important provisions in Measure H to guide the building's rehabilitation. The first was that a fifteen-member Citizens' Advisory Committee be appointed "to review and to advise the City on policies and activities related to the restoration, repair, maintenance, operation, use, promotion and marketing" of the building. The committee was to be formed within thirty days of the effective date of the ordinance created by the passage of the measure, and to maintain its role until June 30, 1999.

The second provision specified that the rehabilitation be consistent with the United States Secretary of the Interior's Standards for Rehabilitating Historic Buildings. These standards consist of ten points based on five principles reflecting historic preservation philosophy: minimal intervention; maintenance of integrity and authenticity; research and documentation; compatibility (visual and physical); and reversibility. The Secretary's Standards were the committee's and the design/build team's court of resort for all questions regarding the appropriateness of any given action.

That the authors of Measure H were astute in their crafting of the ordinance is reflected in the successful completion of the auditorium's rehabilitation.

and instead select a design and construction team, headed by a contracting firm, to operate the project on a design/build basis. The committeee and staff identified the minimum scope of work by listing the items that needed to be included, then listed things that they would like to have done if the budget allowed for it.

In September 1994, the city issued a request for proposals, and a selection committee, including two members of the CAC, chose the Turner Construction team for the project. In addition to Turner, the team consisted of KMD Architects of San Francisco, Oshima and Yee of Sacramento, and the engineering firms of EQE International, Harry A. Yee and Associates, and Capital Engineering Consultants. The historical building fabric and character were under the watchful eye of Historic Environment Consultants. With the help of the city staff, the CAC would now turn its attention to overseeing the project and making sure that the provisions of Measure H were followed.

The auditorium fenced and signed, similar to the Mary J. Watson School in November 1924 when it was under demolition. *John Snyder.*

A RETURN TO ITS FORMER GLORY

O ver a period of perhaps forty years prior to its 1986 closure, the city had been discussing some type of rehabilitation, expansion, or remodeling of the auditorium. What to do, how much to spend, and where to get the money had been recurring community topics, as well as the subject of numerous news articles, and several architectural studies and proposals. There were plans in 1944 to enlarge the building for veterans' uses right after World War II. Later, a 1960s proposal placed the auditorium in the middle of an expanded Convention Center complex, interconnected with two other large buildings. The conversion of the auditorium to a fixed-seat theater was the most extensive and costly of the plans proposed for the building after its closure and created a major controversy that led to a community vote as to the fate of the Auditorium (Measure H).

After the passage of Measure H and the subsequent unavailability of the bond issue funds, the concept that guided the rehabilitation of the auditorium was the practical question of money. In short, the City Council wanted the least expensive project it could get, limiting rehab funds stringently to just that work necessary to re-open the building. Repairing many significant elements of the building that had been damaged or deteriorated over time was considered to be beyond the scope of the project. Lack of main-

tenance following the auditorium's closure also contributed to the work that now had become necessary to open the building to the public. Seismic retrofit needs and the Americans with Disabilities Act (ADA) requirements also increased the work program.

In its final scope of services for the auditorium, the city outlined twenty-nine items that absolutely needed to be undertaken to open the doors. These became the work program for Turner Construction Company and its sub-contractors.

The twenty-nine items included the following:

• Repair and seismically strengthen the decorative plaster ceiling of the main auditorium;

• Upgrade entries, graphics and signage, restrooms, telephones, drinking fountains, one ticket booth, and handicap access ramps to conform to ADA requirements;

• Repair and clean upper and lower balcony seats, provide refurbished, reupholstered seats in the Dress Circle, and replace ceiling under lower balcony;

• Remove some upper balcony seats to provide cross aisles for conformance to building occupancy and fire codes;

• Repair and repaint mirrored dressing rooms flanking the stage, provide one with handicap access;

156

- Provide new electrical service, replace existing switchboard, install emergency generator, and refurbish existing lobby, corridor and main arena lighting;

- Install new fire alarm and sprinkler system with sensitivity to historic fabric and architectural values;

- Refurbish, reuse, and enhance heating, ventilation, and air conditioning (HVAC)systems;

- Refurbish the sound and theatrical lighting systems;

- Prepare and paint existing exterior painted surfaces and interior walls in public areas and replace corridor ceilings;

- Clean and repair proscenium arch and adjacent decorative wall surfaces, columns, and organ screens;

- Refurbish existing memorial in main lobby and create and install a new memorial to all veterans in Memorial Hall.

This list of items, however, did not tell the whole story. The ceilings of the corridors and balcony overhang had been previously removed in order to discard the noise-deadening asbestos-laden acoustical plaster. The removal had damaged the gilded plaster rope trim under the balcony. The painted cast plaster work of the main foyer entrance to the auditorium space had also been damaged by asbestos removal. Further, since the building had been painted with lead-based paint commonly used prior to the 1970s, lead abatement work also became a requirement.

The design/build team's creative solutions to difficult problems in a number of situations not only saved city funds but saved original building fabric and ornament as well. For instance, seismically strengthening the suspended decorative plaster ceiling without either removing and replacing it or embedding visible support hardware was a major challenge to the structural engineers. They chose a solution they had used on a similar ceiling in the San Francisco War Memorial Opera House after the Loma Prieta earthquake. They noted that after that event, interior damage had occurred mainly where the walls met the ceiling, creating torsional stresses. To remediate the situation, they made a thin horizontal cut around the perimeter of the ceiling at its junction with vertical walls or supports, freeing the suspended ceiling from its connection to the walls, and thus from the potential for seismic stress. An additional 70 tons of structural steel reinforcement was added to the existing steel and to the ceiling trusses and cross beams above.

In order to get the large steel beams into the attic, engineers originally thought that they would need to remove part of the roof, possibly during part of

A removable ceiling rosette lined with sheet metal provided a way to lift steel pieces into the attic to reinforce the ceiling.
Ed Andersen.

the rainy season. However, earlier modifications had resulted in the removal of a few of the plaster ceiling rosettes or coffers—possibly to allow circus performers to descend into the auditorium through the ceiling or additional sound equipment to be lowered, and removable painted wood "rosette" imitations had been laid over the openings in their place. These already modified openings proved to be the answer to the problem. The contractors set one of covers aside, lined the opening with protective sheet metal collars, and raised the steel beams one at a time from the auditorium floor, through the opening, and into the attic. A crane type of hoist in the attic was used to hoist the steel.

Shear walls were installed in the north walls of the Little Theater and Memorial Hall, as well as in the east and west walls of the back stage area.

Some of the ductwork of the original heating and air circulation system was retained, but the direction of the air flow was reversed. The supply air now flows through ducts overhead and down through the ceiling. The return air is drawn through the "mushroom caps" beneath the seats and ultimately into the basement for recirculation to the attic. With the installation of a new boiler, the huge fans connected to giant radiators (heat transfer units) were all removed from the basement. New efficient copper coils and energy-efficient HVAC units were installed.

Special research was initiated to determine the original interior color scheme. Preservation professionals sanded and "cratered" painted surfaces throughout the building to reveal the colors of the different layers of paint beneath. Starting with the original first or lowest coat, and working toward the most recent layer, the layers of paint were identified and color-matched to both a professional standard and to contemporary paint company samples. Approximately twenty-two surfaces were sanded and analyzed. The now-revealed original color scheme was used to guide the selection of colors for the rehabilitation. However, since many of the surfaces in the auditorium had originally been variegated or glazed, later overpainting had obscured their original color and character, limiting information and escalating potential reproduction costs. Without actual examples, reproduction of original glazing and tinting techniques would have been conjectural, and so the overpainted surfaces were simply repainted.

Photographic research illustrated changes over time, such as the first overpainting of the originally faux-

158

marbled column bases and organ screens with a solid color. The research also revealed that the walls at the end of the Dress Circle and the walls flanking the stage at the balcony level, originally "marbled," had later been painted a flat, lighter color.

Fortunately, several original doors in the building, particularly those leading to closets and checkrooms, had not been overpainted on the inside surface, and these provided a guide to the actual color and antiquing technique originally used to simulate copper or bronze doors. During the rehabilitation, the team painted the interior doors a composite of the colors used in the original antiquing process.

The contractor cleaned, refurbished, and rewired the original light fixtures in the lobby, main auditorium, and corridors. The team brought in the craftsmen who had originally designed the fixtures to replicate any that were missing.

In order to repair and clean the large interior ceiling, workers erected a huge scaffolding system in the balconies, with a free-standing and movable, fifty-foot-tall segment that they could roll around in the center of the arena. The impressive scaffold, also used to clean, repair, and touch up the proscenium arches and gild the column capitals, would have been the envy of Michaelangelo!

On the exterior, the installation of the cooling tower replaced some camellias that had been placed in the planting areas. A simple ramp with a metal pipe rail was installed on the southeast side of the facade of the building to provide handicapped access to the building.

The construction workers shared an enthusiasm and appreciation for the building that they spread into the community as unofficial ambassadors. There are many special stories. The man assigned to frame up a simple doorway to the new wheelchair lift to the dressing rooms, took the initiative of giving the doorway an arched top, so it would be more in keeping with the rest of the building. Workers who filled in a gap between an original concrete block wall and a new fire door scored the surface of the new material to resemble the texture of the old wall. It is not a public area, but they felt it should match.

As work progressed, new issues arose, and perspectives and proposed work orders were changed. New information came to light as team members delved into the far corners of the building and "discovered things." The resulting sheaf of change orders modified the original program for the better. Principal Turner Construction Company on-site staff members, Terry Richards, Harry Smith, Kairee Waters, and Don Humphries, and architects, Kaplan, McLaughlin, Diaz, of San Francisco, Oshima and Yee, of Sacramento, and Paula Boghosian of Historic Environment Consultants closely coordinated their efforts with

159

City staff, Mike George and Leonard Zerilli. In spite of the continual discovery of yet something else that needed replacing or to be done differently (and usually more expensively) than anticipated, this approach resulted in achieving the high quality of work evident in the completed job. Of course, with such limited available funding, each expenditure was thoroughly scrutinized.

As this ambitious project evolved, everyone connected with it again and again provided extra service, extra concern, and extra care. Professionals, city staff, contractors, craftsmen, and technicians all shared the same goal, to restore the glory of the auditorium, to recreate the "feeling" and intent of Dean's original design, and to bring this grand old dowager, shimmering again, into the twenty-first century.

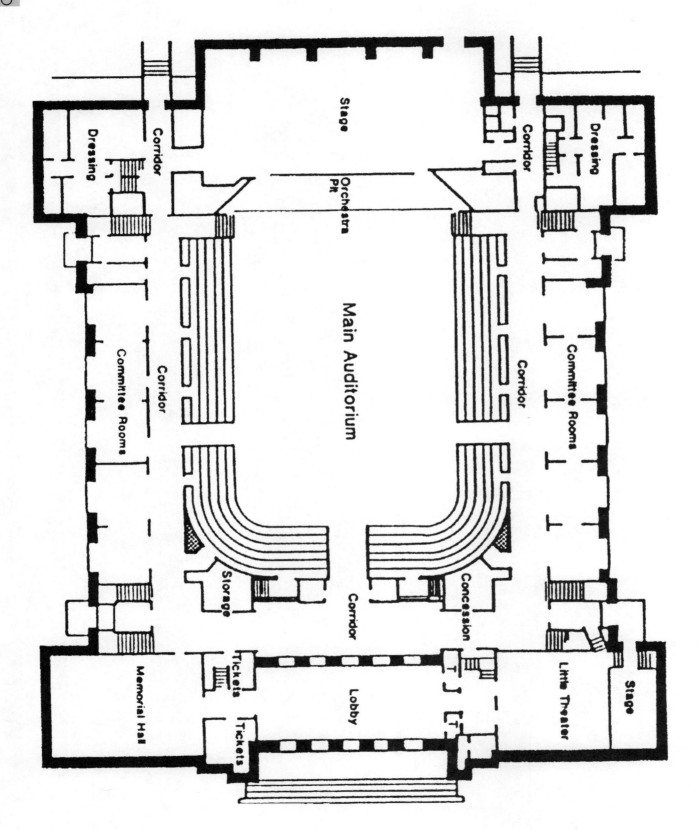

Sheets of gold leaf were pressed onto the capitals. When the excess was brushed away, gold remained only on the high areas giving a sense of depth to the design.
Ed Andersen.

The enormous movable scaffolding used to repair and re-glaze the ceiling took seven workers to shift.
Don Tateishi.

The archway leading to the main hall was completely regilded and stenciled. *Paula Boghosian.*

Skilled artisans reglaze ceiling atop movable scaffold. *Ed Andersen.*

The finished hall just before opening weekend. *Doug Austin.*

Restoring the Decoratively Painted Surfaces

The ceiling and the proscenium wall, arch, and supporting columns are the most decorative part of the auditorium, but for many years layers of smoke residue obscured the richness of this decoration. During the recent rehabilitation, skilled professionals from Evergreene Painting of New York City restored these surfaces to their former glory.

In addition to the coating of smoke, the ceiling had cracked and spalling plaster, and peeling paint. The Evergreene crew removed all the loose paint and plaster, repaired the cracks, then repainted and re-glazed the entire surface from a huge rolling scaffolding that took seven workers to move. The original pierced centers of the ceiling coffers had been covered over in 1937 with like pieces that were sturdier and more sound absorbing. These had been attached with plaster and were left in place, as removing them would have destroyed the original elements behind them.

Although not appearing to be gold-leafed, the richness of the wall and arch is the result of having a layer of gold leaf under the stenciled design. The original decorators, A. T. Heinsbergen of Los Angeles, first painted the wall in bright yellow-green. Over that background color, they applied the gold leaf. Over the gold leaf, they applied the stencil designs, and then the whole was varnished. The layering gives a depth and richness to the treatment. The Evergreene painters replicated this historical process where the wall required infill painting. In a final step, they sprayed the surfaces with a coating of conservation sealer B67.

Gold leaf, or a composite material of gold and other metals, as was used in the restoration, comes in boxed squares

of very thin foil separated by sheets of tissue. Each sheet of gold is thinner than a strand of human hair. Artisans apply gold leaf by first brushing sizing and glue onto the wall. When the glue has dried to just the right degree of tackiness, they carefully lay the square sheet of gold leaf, with the tissue still in place, on the prepared surface. They then go over the surface with a fine brush to ensure adherence and remove any gold leaf particles.

The sheets are applied side by side, creating a grid-like pattern. When no stenciling or painting is put over gold leaf, the pattern of squares is very apparent. Such a pattern can be seen on the soffit of the arch in the auditorium. This one, however, is the result of the original craftsmen cheating, probably to save money. The artisans applied the gold leaf in smaller pieces, not whole squares. Then, to make it look as though it had been laid in squares, they painted a grid pattern over the gold leaf using a transparent glaze. It was very effective, especially since is it nearly always viewed from fifty feet below.

The arch over the door to the auditorium was completely re-done. Because funds for rehabilitation were so limited, decisions as to what should be included were always carefully considered. The arch had become nicked and chipped over the years, but when the asbestos was removed from the ceiling and the new surface reapplied, the arch suffered greatly along the top edge: The surface was pulled off down to the white plaster layer. Co-author Paula Boghosian, the preservation consultant on Turner's design/build team, repeatedly urged that this arch, with its commanding location, be made a priority. Her frequent pleas on its behalf caused the design/build team, with the city's consent, not only to include the doorway element in the budget, but to dub it "Paula's Arch."

The budget allowed for the arch to be cleaned, repaired, and in-painted where necessary. However, after examining the arch closely, the Evergreene company principals and staff felt that this would not give it the best appearance. They therefore decided to restore the entire surface, at no extra charge. To restore "Paula's Arch," Armand Herreras, the Evergreene artisan, first carefully traced the stenciled design and created a new template from it. Next he painted over the whole area, applied new gold leaf in perfect squares, and re-stenciled the design. Finally, Herreras applied a layer of tinted varnish to both protect and give depth and definition to the decoration.

The decorative motifs molded into the capitals of the columns supporting the proscenium arch were designed expressly for their location and with the memorial intent of the building in mind. Upon close inspection the able eye can discern the letter "S" for Sacramento and military symbols such as cannons, bullets, ships' wheels, and anchors. Eagles are placed at the front edges, and owls span the area between the capitals. These magnificent pieces of work were re-gold-leafed in a technique called "tipping." To enhance

their deep modeling, the artisan applied the sizing and glue only to the high portions. After laying the sheets of gold over the glue, he brushed away whatever did not adhere, leaving the recessed areas untouched, and accentuating their depth.

The rope molding below the balcony was replaced in areas where it was severely damaged during the asbestos abatement and re-surfacing of the adjacent plaster. Although it was originally gold leafed, cost prohibited restoring it in that manner. Instead, it was carefully painted with metallic gold sign paint and glazed. Overspray from adhesive, perhaps that used when the asbestos was attached, had covered and damaged the glazed soffit between the ropes in many areas. In addition, initials had been burned into the surface with cigarette lighters. Herreras cleaned off the adhesive and patched the damaged areas on the front portion of the soffit and completely redid the painting and glazing on the back portion.

Herreras, who has restored painting in fifteen theaters, was especially pleased to work on the auditorium, because before his employment with Evergreene, he worked for the company that did the original decorating. The Heinsbergen company was taken over by the original owner's son upon his father's death but closed in 1990. Herreras considers that his work on the building has been part of a continuum of the original craftsman's effort.

EPILOGUE

Eager crowd assembled in anticipation of opening ceremonies. *Doug Austin.*

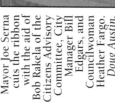

Mayor Joe Serna cuts the ribbon with the aid of Bob Rakela of the Citizens Advisory Committee, City Manager Bill Edgars, and Councilwoman Heather Fargo. *Doug Austin.*

I'm so glad I took Grandma to the re opening of the Memorial Auditorium today. I meant it to be for her, since she had told me so many times about all the wonderful things she had gone to there and about going to the first opening in 1927. But the day turned out to be for me, too.

The first thing I noticed when we pulled up and parked the car was the red carpet that went from the street right up to the front door. Someone said that it had been put there for the grand opening gala the night before, but it seemed to me that it was there to give all Sacramentans a grand "welcome back." We could have cut across the lawn, but I steered Grandma down the sidewalk so we could walk the whole length of that carpet. I had never walked up a red carpet before and I wasn't going to miss the chance.

Near the entrance we stopped in the crowd and watched the mayor and a councilwoman cut a red ribbon strung across the doorway with a huge pair of scissors. There were some speeches that I don't remember much about, then dozens of white doves were released. When they all took off at once their flapping wings made an almost explosive sound. They seemed to actually leap into the air, then they

Balloons and white doves rose, nearly simultaneously, to the sky. *Doug Austin.*

Doug Austin.

raced back and forth and flew off. As the doves were circling hundreds of red, yellow and blue balloons rose below them. I really got caught up in the spirit of the event watching those balloons swirl up to the sky. After that some World War I veterans, dressed in their old uniforms, fired a cannon they said used to sit next to the steps. It made a thunderous boom that startled Grandma even though she was expecting it.

After the ceremonies, Grandma and I moved with the crowd through the front doors of the auditorium. It wasn't long before Grandma ran into a lady she had gone to high school with. They had graduated right here in the Memorial Auditorium! It was fun to listen to their memories of that night and of the other kids they went to school with. After a while, I left them to their remembrances and went into the main lobby. Right in front of me was this gorgeous archway that was painted a bright gold. As I stood admiring the arch, I heard a woman

standing nearby say in a quiet voice, "I fell in love here for the very first time, at a high school dance." At first I thought she was speaking into the hall in general, then a subtle sideways glance told me that she was also directing her words to me, and I noticed a look in her eyes that made me think that, for a few seconds, she was back in that moment again.

A dark-haired woman standing on the other side of her said that she and her sister had taken tap dancing over at the Clunie Clubhouse and performed during the Christmas shows here. I told them that my dad had brought me here to see "Sesame Street Live" once, but I was only five at the time and really didn't remember much about the building. But I said Dad told me that he had come to a Loggins & Messina concert here in the late '70s, and that it was one of the best concerts he ever went to.

Then a man on my right, who had been listening, commented that he appeared here in a school play back in 1964, but his best memory was seeing Bobby Chacon fight Bazooka Limon for the championship. I guess they must have been boxers, because he threw a couple of punches into the air as he said it. When I laughed, he smiled at me and winked.

I decided to leave my group of new-found friends to go see how Grandma was doing. I found her and her old friend still out in the foyer. She called me over then grabbed my arm and pulled me close to her side. Her friend pointed an arthritic finger up at the wall where a bunch of names were imprinted in brass letters. In her crackly old voice she said, "That's my uncle's name up there." She told us that he was her mother's brother and was killed in World War I. She was just a baby then, but when she grew up, her mother used to tell her about him. She said they built this building to honor the soldiers who died in World War I. Then she took us into the room at the left of the lobby and showed us where they had put plaques with the names of all the people from Sacramento who died in any of our wars. She and Grandma liked that idea.

After that we walked back across the lobby and looked in the Little Theater. It was still all dirty and in disrepair. A guide told us that they didn't have enough money to fix it up, but they hope to be able to soon. I thought that theater was really cool. Maybe when they get it fixed, up I'll be in a play there someday.

As we walked back into the lobby, we heard some music coming from the main hall. Grandma and I were anxious to see it, so we went in through the doors under the gold arch. I was amazed when we got inside. The band was pretty good, but I couldn't take my eyes off all the painting and decorations in the room. What a beautiful place! The wall around the stage sparkled with jewel-like colors and gold paint. The huge columns on either side of the stage had bright gold capitals. Colored lights were shining

up at the columns and made the area behind them bright red. The ceiling way above us was all painted in different colors and had a soft glow. Grandma said the kind of finish that was on it is called a glaze finish. It's what they used to do a lot back then, and it was just like she remembered it. I thought it was totally cool.

The main lobby of the newly rehabilitated auditorium on opening day. *Doug Austin.*

166

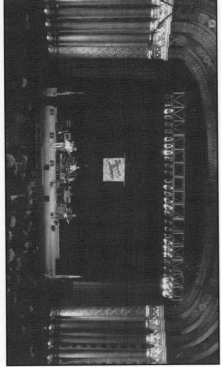

The rehabilitated main hall as seen from under an arch of balloons. *Doug Austin.*

Tangle James was one of numerous groups to entertains guests on the opening weekend. *Doug Austin.*

We rested in there for a while and watched some other cool acts, then we left and walked down one of the side halls. There was a display of military stuff that we looked at for a while, and Grandma explained some of the different styles of uniforms to me. Next to that was a display of historical photographs. One of them was of a dance pageant put on by Sacramento City College—but it wasn't called that back then—and Grandma recognized some of her friends in the picture.

I heard a young woman near me tell one of the ladies behind the table that her great-grandfather had helped make the bricks for the auditorium. She seemed pretty proud of that. I don't blame her, I would be, too. Then I saw

an old man bent over one of the tables filling out a form for a time capsule in shaky handwriting. I noticed he wrote that he had graduated from Sacramento High School here in the auditorium in 1934! I moved closer to see what else he was writing. He put down that he was born in Sacramento and had watched the construction of this building. He was also initiated into the "Fraternal Order of Eagles" in 1937 with 500 other men. I moved down the line a ways, peeking over other shoulders. One woman wrote that she hoped to see her grandchildren graduate here like she had! She said they are fourth generation Sacramentans—so am I!

I left Grandma looking at the pictures and reminiscing with the others and walked back into the main hall. I found an empty seat and slumped into it. A singing group was on the stage this time, and I listened for a while, then hunkered down and began to think about the place. I used to feel Grandma was overly sentimental when she talked about the auditorium and the memories she had of it. But now I see she wasn't. Lots of other people obviously feel the same way. Thinking about what I had heard over that last hour or so, I realized that what was happening there wasn't just about a building or events. It was about the people whose lives had been changed here. The auditorium was their place and nobody could take it away from them. Grandma calls it the campfire of our people. After today, I feel like it's my

Approximately 20,000 people attended the grand re-opening of the Memorial Auditorium during the two-day event on November 10 and 11, 1996. *Doug Austin.*

place too. Sharing this day with Grandma has put my spirit in there as well.

Sitting in that big room, I could sense all the ghosts of the past moving about. I felt connected to all those who had come before me. I think when they closed the auditorium ten years ago, the old ghosts never left it. It was everyone else who left. But they have come back now, and I'm glad, because now I will have a chance to gather my own memories there, like Grandma and all those other people.

With the floor in its tilted position for theater seating, the orchestra pit, missing its curtain, was visible during re-opening ceremonies. *Doug Austin.*

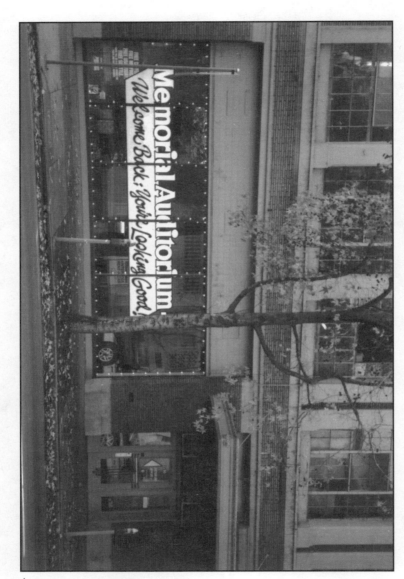

Daugherty
Downtown Service
and Parts store
across the street
from the Memorial
Auditorium
painted a welcome
sign on their
window.
John Snyder.

Appendix

NOTES

Chapter 1 - The Stage is Set

1. R. H. Hunt, "The Designing of Auditoriums," *The Architectural Forum*, September 1927. General reference: Historic Environment Consultants, Sacramento Non-Residential Building Survey, 1981.

Chapter 2 - Nurturing an Idea

1. Myrtle Shaw Lord, *A Sacramento Saga: Fifty Years of Achievement - Chamber of Commerce Leadership*, Sacramento: Sacramento Chamber of Commerce, 1946, pp. 209-210. *The Sacramento Bee* 6/1/16. 2. *The Sacramento Bee* 11/19/18. 3. *The Sacramento Bee* 11/19/18. 4. *The Sacramento Bee* 11/20/18. 5. *The Sacramento Bee* 11/19/21; Edith E. Pitti, "Background to the Construction of the Memorial Auditorium, 1918-1927," Unpublished MS 1986, pp. 25, 31. 6. *The Sacramento Bee* 11/11/22. 7. *The Sacramento Bee* 12/2/22. 8. *The Sacramento Bee* 4/27/23. 9. *The Sacramento Bee* 11/19/21. 10. *The Sacramento Bee* 5/30/23. General references: *The Sacramento Bee* 3/25/13; 8/12/16; 11/19/18; 12/23/18; 10/14/21; 11/17/21; 5/4/22; 5/2/23; 5/23/23; 6/19/23; 12/21/23; Lord pp. 96, 341; Susan M. Strauss, Sacramento Memorial Auditorium History Study, prepared by James Stewart Polshek and Partners and Dreyfuss Blackford Architects for the City of Sacramento, pp. 7, 10. City Council Records vol. 30, pp. 230-231, May 31, 1923.

Chapter 3 - Getting Down to Business

1. *The Sacramento Bee* 9/22/23. 2. *The Sacramento Bee* 11/28/24. 3. *The Sacramento Bee* 6/19/25. 4. *The Sacramento Bee* 6/
24/25. 5. *The Sacramento Bee* 6/25/25. 6. *The Sacramento Bee* 7/16/25. General references: *The Sacramento Bee* 1/4/24; 2/8/24; 7/17/24; 8/22/24; 7/17/27. Strauss pp. 18-20.

Chapter 4 - Bricks and Mortar

1. *The Sacramento Bee* 10/24/25. General references: *The Sacramento Bee* 9/4/24; 9/23/25; 9/24/25; 10/6/25; 10/14/25; 10/31/25; 11/18/25; 12/16/25; 1/20/26; 5/11/26; 5/15/26; 5/28/26; 7/17/26; 10/16/26; 12/25/26; 1/21/27.

Chapter 5 - All Its Glory

1. *The Sacramento Bee* 2/21/27.

The Little Theater

1. *The Sacramento Bee* 6/19/23. 2. *The Sacramento Bee* 2/21/27.

Chapter 6 - Pride of Accomplishment

1. *The Sacramento Bee* 2/21/27. 2. *The Sacramento Bee* 2/21/27. 3. *The Sacramento Bee* 2/21/27. 4. *The Sacramento Bee* 2/21/27. 5. *The Sacramento Bee* 2/21/27. 6. *The Sacramento Bee* 2/21/27. 7. *The Sacramento Bee* 2/21/27. General Reference: *The Sacramento Bee* 2/24/27.

The Organ

General references: *The Sacramento Bee* 3/20/24; 11/28/24; 11/13/25.

The Chimes

General references: *The Sacramento Bee* 7/18/23; 5/26/26; 5/28/26.

Chapter 7 - Decade One: 1927-1937

1. *The Sacramento Bee* 11/2/28. 2. *The Sacramento Bee* 1/24/30. 3. *The Sacramento Bee* 3/16/28. 4. *The Sacramento Bee* 2/25/29. 5. *The Sacramento Bee* 2/27/29. General References: *The Sacramento Bee* 5/25/27; 6/23/27; 9/5/27; 3/19/28; 10/30/28; 2/16/29; 4/18/29; 8/9/29; 11/8/29; 1/4/33; 1/26/33; 4/7/33; 4/14/33; 12/30/35; 2/11/36.

Chapter 8 - Decade Two: 1937-1947

1. *The Sacramento Bee* 5/2/42. General References: *The Sacramento Bee* 4/5/34; 4/10/34; 4/15/34; 4/8/43; 5/7/43; 5/9/43; 5/11/43; 5/12/43; 3/2/44; 8/3/44; 8/4/44; 8/16/44; 10/19/44; 10/20/44; 10/24/44; 10/30/44. *The Sacramento Union* 1/5/44.

Chapter 9 - Decade Three: 1947-195

General references: *The Sacramento Bee* 5/21/48; 6/4/48; 2/20/52; 12/19/55; 1/4/57; 2/23/57.

Camellia Festival

General reference: F. Melvyn Lawson, *Flower Power: the Story of the Sacramento Camellia Festival,* Sacramento: Sacramento Camellia Festival, 1989.

Chapter 10 - Decade Four: 1957-1967

1. *The Sacramento Union* 10/7/59. 2. *The Sacramento Union* 1/5/60. General references: *The Sacramento Bee* 7/11/57; 7/12/57; 7/4/58; 7/10/58; 7/24/58; 8/6/58; 9/17/58; 9/25/58; 9/29/58; 10/5/59; 1/8/60; 2/1/67. *The Sacramento Union* 10/5/59; 1/5/60; 1/8/60; 1/20/67. Memorial Auditorium Maintenance Records. Convention Bureau material.

Chapter 11 - Decade Five: 1967-1977

General references: *The Sacramento Bee* 1/9/76; 9/18/76. *The Sacramento Union* 7/8/71.

Chapter 12 - Decade Six: 1977-1987

1. *The Sacramento Bee* 4/8/80. 2. *The Sacramento Bee* 3/6/86. 3. *The Sacramento Bee* 3/6/86. General references: *The Sacramento Bee* 10/18/77; 8/29/78; 12/18/83; 2/16/86; 2/19/86; 1/15/86. *The Sacramento Union* 4/27/83.

You Can't Hear Anything in That Big Barn

1. *The Sacramento Bee* 12/19/55. 2. *The Sacramento Bee* 4/16/66. General references: *The Sacramento Bee* 8/11/27; 2/11/36; 6/30/37; 4/26/41; 2/20/52; 12/12/53.

Chapter 13 - Decade Seven: 1987-1997

General reference: *The Sacramento Bee* 4/9/88.

Round One!

1. *The Sacramento Bee* 5/21/48. 2. *The Sacramento Bee* 5/21/48.

People Who Helped

Ed Andersen
Nicoletta Anselmo
Doug Austin
Willi Bagdasarian
Peter Basofin
Sharon Blixt
Stan Bollinger
Judith Browne
Kevin Bunker
Ruth O'Kane Byrne
Neil Calmes
Dorothy Carr
Wally Clark
Dorene Clement
Ralph Congdon
Bill Conlin
Don Cox
John Cox
Barbara Crockett
Grace Taylor Dean
Annette Deglow
Fran Diaz
Bill Estrada
Heather Fargo
Jamie Ferguson
Andy Flink
Lanette Franklin
Janet Galante
Mike George
Bill Glackin
Nate Gourvitch

Dottie Graves
Ron Green
Buddy Harpham
Sherry Hatch
Jim Henley
Armand Herreras
James Herkenroth
Libby Harmor
Marilyn Hornbeck
Jeff Hughson
Jill Hupp
Jim Jayes
Linda Johnson
Pat Johnson
Cal and Hilda Kerfoot
Kay Knepprath
Rich LaVoie
Sookie Lee
Frank Lortie
Frannie Marsellis
Mick Martin
Ruth McCreary
Lissa McKee
Amanda Meeker
Else Meyer
Suzanne Mikesell
Patty Moller
Anne Moore
Mike Moraes
Tom Myers
Scott Nelson
Dennis Neufeld

Charlene Noyes
Denise O'Connor
Josh Pane
Joy Patterson
Violet Phelps
Mahlon Picht
Betty Jane Powell
Bob Rakela
Bill Rase
Ken Robbins
Dixie Robertson
Anne Rudin
Greg Savalin
Francesca Smith
John Snyder
Mike Stauffer
Frank Stimson
Hulda Stone
Fran Summer
Harry Sweet
Don Tateishi
Sid Tenner
Don Tognotti
Rich Tolmach
Nick Tomich
Cindy Unmack
Fred Vail
John Webre
Dennis Warren
Tom Winter
Leonard Zerilli

MEMORIAL AUDITORIUM AT A GLANCE

BUILDING STATISTICS

Overall dimensions: 216 feet wide, 215 feet long, main building: 80 feet high, towers: 100 feet high. Auditorium space: 108 x 175 clear span. Roof: supported on two main steel trusses 176 feet long. Stage: 40 feet deep, 100 feet wide. Three hundred and forty thousand decoratively finished bricks were used in the building.

A special feature was the tilting arena floor, which drops four feet at the front and rises slightly at the back to provide for theater seating. In the lowered position, the orchestra pit is exposed.

Capacity: Auditorium, originally 4600, presently 3500. Little Theater, 300.

Original Cost: $750,000 Bond issue floated by city. Total including furnishings approximately $850,000.

Rehabilitation (Phase I): $10,800,000.

CHRONOLOGY

1910 - Idea first surfaces.

1916 - Chamber of Commerce begins planning.

1918 - Post-war planning begins, idea to make building a memorial to war dead.

1921 - City Council appoints committee.

1922 - Local organizations pledge support for construction of auditorium.

May 16, 1923 - Bond issue for $750,000 passes.

May 21, 1923 - City Council approves 16th and J Street site.

1924 - Architects hired, James Dean appointed City Architect.

July 1924 - Preliminary plans revealed to public.

November 1924 - Mary J. Watson School demolished to make way for auditorium.

May 1925 - City gets legal judgment validating 16th and J Street site.

July 16, 1925 - Groundbreaking ceremony.

October 5, 1925 - General contract let to Mathews Construction.

May 15, 1926 - Cornerstone placed.

January 31, 1927 - City officials inspect completed building.

February 22, 1927 - Grand opening.

February 27, 1927 - First noncommunity event held in building (San Carlo Opera Company's performance of *Aida*).

March 7, 1927 - First performance in Little Theater.

March 30, 1927 - First organ concert.

September 26, 1958 - City holds Auditorium Weekend to celebrate completion of two-month closure for renovations.

November 17, 1977 - Building nominated to the National Register of Historic Places.

February 5, 1986 - Last rock concert held before ten-year closure.

March 9, 1986 - City locks doors behind Folk Dance Festival and appoints 19-member task force to determine auditorium's future.

July 30, 1986 - Task Force votes to turn auditorium into fixed-seat theater.

May 7, 1987 - City Council approves Task Force's recommendation.

February 1991 - Fixed-seat theater remodel plans revealed to public.

March 18, 1991 - Sacramento Old City Association members tour auditorium.

July 3, 1991 - Save the Auditorium! committee (STA!) files voter initiative (Measure H) with City Clerk.

January 1992 - STA! turns over 33,000 signatures to city clerk.

November 1992 - Measure H passes by 221 votes.

1993 - Mayor Anne Rudin appoints Citizens' Advisory Committee to carry out rehabilitation according to Measure H.

June 21, 1994 - City Council approves two-step process for selection of Construction and Design team.

August 29, 1994 - City puts out Request for Proposals (RFP) for rehabilitation.

November 1994 - City awards contract to Turner Construction.

November 28, 1995 - Design is completed, construction begins.

November 10-11, 1996 - Rehabilitated auditorium re-opens. 20,000 people attend two-day event.